Unfailing Grace

How Adversity Magnifies The Grace Within
Showing The Beauty Of This Tapestry Of Life

Julie Carrick

Foreword by Kitty Cleveland

Unless otherwise noted, all scriptures are from the JERUSALEM BIBLE Copyright© 1966, 1967, 1968 by Darton, Longmand & Todd LTD and Doubleday and Co. Inc. All rights reserved.

Publishing Services provided by Paper Raven Books

Printed in the United States of America

First Printing, 2019

Hardcover ISBN 978-1-7334343-0-0
Paperback ISBN 978-1-7334343-1-7

This book is dedicated to Kurt Carrick,
my husband and best friend.

To Father John Szydlowski for baptizing me into a life of grace
and introducing me to Jesus in the Eucharist; and to Father
Joseph Battersby for demonstrating the tender way grace
can be "sipped" every day.

To my grandmothers, Julia Karas and Frances Edel, for their
daily examples of grace in their deed and their
gently whispered prayer.

To my dear Barbara Beatty for being friend, sister,
fairy godmother, and guardian of grace.

And saving the best for last, to blessed Mama Mary.
You all fully prove God's unfailing grace.

Foreword

Julie Carrick and I met almost 20 years ago in Washington D.C., where we were both attending the UCMVA Unity Awards (the equivalent of the "Catholic Grammys") at the Hartke Theater. I had just released my first CD of Christian music and was new to this whole world of recording, but I knew that I had finally found my tribe.

I first heard Julie's angelic singing voice during the celebration of Mass at the hotel when she led the worship with her guitar. I introduced myself afterwards and said, "You have an *anointing!*" How true that statement was. And it's become even more evident as I've watched her overcome numerous struggles and setbacks over the years with grace, courage, and unwavering faith, all while singing God's praises.

Julie and I became fast friends when she accepted my invitation to come to Louisiana and put on a concert at my home church in Mandeville. Though I had already released a CD and had some media exposure, I'd only given one concert up to that point! I knew that I had a lot to learn and that Julie had a lot she could teach me. True to form, she graciously did that (and so much more).

It's in that spirit of generosity that Julie has written *Unfailing Grace*, which takes an unflinching look at the way the Lord Jesus has ministered to her—and through her—in times of profound loss and adversity. We will all suffer, it's true, but what an encouragement it is to see someone embrace her cross with faith and then share with us the hope and promise of resurrection on the other end (and to back it up with beautiful music to boot!).

My prayer is that these pages will resonate with you and encourage you as you navigate your own struggles and setbacks in this gift of life. Open your heart to what she has to share, both in word and in song, and allow the Holy Spirit to speak truth and life into every place that needs healing and restoration.

Finally, if you don't yet have a relationship with Mary, the Mother of Jesus (and your spiritual mother, whether you know it or not), I want you to be open to being pleasantly surprised. Julie shares in this book how Mary has had a powerful role to play in her own journey towards Heaven, and she has a powerful role to play in your life as well.

May God bless you and give you his abiding peace,

Kitty Cleveland

Introduction

L ike me, have you ever asked yourself, "Is God interested in my life?" Or, "If God loves me, why am I allowed to experience such deep pain in my life?" Or, "Why does God allow my loved ones to go through so many trials?" I hope as you read the stories from my life, you will see reflected in them the stories of your own.

We know that our lives are not just stories. They are made up of real experiences and relationships, times of discovery and trial, moments of triumphs and deep sorrows. How we allow these experiences to abide in us makes the difference.

There is one relationship that is eternal: our bond with God. At times, this relationship is a real struggle. Depending on what we are going through in a given moment or life experience, we may even ask if God is real.

I am reminded of a line in the movie *The Count of Monte Cristo.* The dying priest and the man wrongfully charged with treason and imprisoned for life spent those last precious moments together in a prison cell. The wrongfully accused man said, "I don't believe in God!" The priest simply replied, "That doesn't matter. He believes in you."

I know that God believes in me. As you read this book, I pray the events of my life will help you see that God believes in you, too. Not only does he believe in you, but he also loves you beyond all telling.

Being raised a cradle Catholic and living this faith my entire life, I will be sharing my stories from that perspective. But whether you are Catholic, Protestant, Jewish, or still trying to find the answer as to who God is, or if he is, I hope that this book will help you to find that kinship. Our belief or unbelief of this phenomenal deity does not make him any less or any more real. He just is. And he is just in love with you.

Prayer is the way we communicate with God. The more we are in daily conversation with him, the more we see that he is present in all the details of our lives. We think that if we are close to God and pray every day, we will be spared sadness, disappointments, and trials. The reality is that while we are north of the daisies, living and breathing, we will experience life in every possible way. God is here with us in the very midst of it. He knows what we will go through and until we are with him in eternity, he allows his grace to give us the strength we need to live each day.

Be sure to download a QR code reader if you don't already have one.

As a recording artist, singer-songwriter, and composer, I have written songs over these years that share my heart and my experiences. Some are ridiculously joy filled when I have realized the magnitude of God's love for me. Others are introspective and show the deep emotions that naturally occur in other realities that I have survived. Throughout this book, I have included a way for you to listen to some of the songs that I have written. The lyrics are printed in the various chapters along with a QR code that you can scan and literally listen to each song. Technology can be lovely at times.

This book is not about the life of a recording artist, but the life of a person who loves God and relies on his unfailing grace to someday bring me home to him. Before we begin, I just want to say thank you to my husband, Kurt. I have an amazing husband. He has allowed me to share our journey. Many people would not want to be as revealing as we shall be, but unless you know the whole story, you would not really see just how powerful grace is when we need it most. When I share what we have been through, I ask you to bear in mind the phrase, "The devil wouldn't tempt you if you weren't a worthy prize." I am also grateful to Janice and Rhett. Your friendship and guidance are gifts of grace, and I constantly thank God that he introduced us to each other. Who knew breakfast would be where I would get the answer about all the promptings to write this book?

I know that my life has been a journey of transformative grace. It has taken years to understand and come to fully accept the love that God has for me, even in the darkest moments. But when we can give in to His love, we are literally transformed and no longer despise our dark days. We come to see both the lovely and the harsh realities as the threads of his presence in this tapestry that is our life. God absolutely believes in you and gives you the strength to continue moving toward him day by day. And when we come to accept his unconditional love, we can see him present in so many ways, in every single moment of every single day. We no longer journey alone or in doubt, but find contentment because we see the miracles all around us. The stories that I will share with you can help you see him present in your stories and your journey as well. That is my hope.

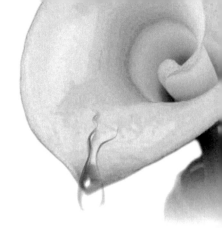

Chapter 1

Several years into our marriage, I heard the words no woman ever wants to hear. My husband and high school sweetheart, Kurt, told me he wanted a divorce. He and one of my closest friends, his assistant, had begun an affair. The betrayal was so deep and so painful I felt like I could not breathe. Pain turned to anger and welled up in me. I saw myself smack my husband across the face. I ran to the bathroom to vomit. It felt like there were creatures in my gut trying to get out.

Next, I ran out of the house and down the block to the apartment of dear friends of ours and told them I needed advice and prayer.

Behind Kurt's eyes was nothing but darkness. He just reiterated that he was in love with this other woman and that was that. I asked him if she had spoken to her husband yet, and he said she was telling him that same night.

I am a Catholic, wife, mother, daughter, sister, friend, recording artist, and speaker. As I share my story, I pray you see where grace, Mama Mary's tender intercession, and clinging to Christ saved my life more than once. I also hope you will see yourself in your own stories. I realize I am known as a recording artist, but what we share in life is so much more than a song. The lyrics and melodies I have written over the years aspire to convey in a more emotional way some of the stories of my life and what I have witnessed over these years.

As a little girl, I remember going to Mass, which is what worship services are called in the Catholic faith. I heard the organ playing, my mother singing, and the choir members looked so happy most of the time. I can still smell the incense in the little church of St. John Cantius in Free Soil, Michigan. Yes, it is a real place. My family—mom, daddy, and my six brothers and sisters— would pile into the station wagon, and we would come home after Sunday Mass for a big, delicious breakfast. They were simple times, and we shared what I thought was a simple faith. But it became the foundation for a powerful grace-filled Catholic faith, and it would make the difference between life and death in so many times to come.

I remember being somewhat jealous of my brothers, who were altar servers. Since they were boys and older than me, they got to serve during Mass as altar boys. They were allowed to walk past the altar rail and stand right next to Father John as he prayed the Mass. I always wanted to do it, but being the little sister, I didn't get to.

Then I had the idea that if I joined the young ladies' sodality in the parish, on Saturdays I would get my chance. This group was made up of young ladies who wanted to learn more about the mother of Jesus and try to emulate her in daily life. So, I used Mama Mary to get closer to her Son. I joined the sodality as early as I could, and the first Saturday that I was in, I showed up early to the church so I could get the feather duster and vacuum cleaner. That way I would be allowed to go up to the rail, open the center gate, and walk right up to the tabernacle, that precious gold cabinet that holds Holy Communion, Jesus. It would take me 20 minutes to dust there.

I think now that perhaps Mama Mary was smiling at little Julie Fran Edel. This was the first time that I really felt Mother Mary close to me. I had learned to pray the Rosary and other beautiful Marian prayers, but this was the first time that she felt so human. I could feel her taking me by the hand and leading me physically closer to Jesus.

Another vivid faith memory that led me from the age of eight to fourteen was the Sacrament of Reconciliation. A Sacrament is a religious ceremony regarded as imparting divine grace, like baptism and the Eucharist. In the Roman Catholic and many Orthodox Churches, reconciliation or confession and the anointing of the sick are beautiful Sacraments. I had studied well in my CCD (Confraternity of Christian Doctrine), or as it is known today, religious education classes, and I was excited to be prepared to receive this gift from our Lord.

I remember lining up with the rest of my classmates in the church, and we waited patiently for our turn to go into the little room and kneel behind the screen. It was finally my turn and

I went in, knelt down, and spoke to Father John Szydlowski. I remember as if it were only yesterday. I made the sign of the cross—marking myself literally in the name of God the Father, in the name Jesus the Son, and in the name of the Holy Spirit—and spoke these words, "Forgive me, Father, for I have sinned. This is my first confession."

Then I very honestly told him, "In thought, I sinned six times. In word, I sinned eight times, and in deed five times."

There was a little pause, and then he asked me if I was sorry for my sins. I said yes. He asked me to say my Act of Contrition prayer.

I learned it well and recited it from memory and in my heart. "Oh my good Jesus, I am heartily sorry for having offended you, whom I love above all. In choosing to do wrong and failing to do good, I have hurt you Jesus, whom I love. With your help, I will go forward to sin no more."

Then he spoke the words of Jesus with such love, "I absolve you in the name of the Father and of the Son and of the Holy Spirit. Now say three Hail Marys in front of the tabernacle and go in peace."

I felt lighter. I felt joyful. I knew I would come to this little room often.

Each Saturday, I would indeed come to the Sacrament of Reconciliation. Every week, I would keep track of my sins and put them into the correct category of thought, word, or deed. I was like a little CPA for Jesus—categorized and accounted for. Joyfully, I would wait my turn in line and then speak to Father John, giving him the correct number of each.

The next Sacrament I received was the precious gift of Jesus in Holy Communion, the Eucharist. When I think about receiving Jesus Christ in the Eucharist, my heart is overwhelmed. To know that he loves me so much that he is willing to literally allow me to hold him inside of me is beyond words. When I see the priest at Mass lift up the bread—Jesus's holy body—and again the chalice—his precious blood—I am brought to tears of overwhelming love as I look upon him whom I am privileged to receive. I can see myself as the little girl trying to get past the altar rail, who at the tender age of nine wore a beautiful white dress and veil as she received him for the first time, while at the same time seeing the grown woman who is still completely in love with Jesus Christ, Lord and Savior.

If there is one Sacrament that has affected me the deepest, it is the Eucharist. To know that Jesus would allow the humble forms of bread and wine to become him fully present is not something that can be explained but needs to be taken in faith by his word. Each time I would go to Mass, I'd fall deeper in love with Christ. I would watch Father John's face as he would gently place the host, Holy Communion, Jesus, on my tongue. He seemed to disappear in the brightness of the beauty of the moment just as much as he became even more present by giving the Eucharist to me.

Then just before my 15th birthday, Father John retired. He moved away to Grand Rapids, Michigan, and the new pastor, Father Joseph Battersby, came to be our priest. The first Saturday he was there, I lined up as usual and went into the confessional and knelt behind the screen. "Forgive me, Father, for I have sinned." I told him exactly how many sins in each category as usual and then there was a pause.

He said, "Excuse me."

So I paused. I said, "Excuse me, Father, for I have sinned."

He said, "Dear, you must tell me your sins."

I said, "I just did that."

He said, "No, for example in deed, what did you do?"

I paused again briefly and thought about why he was asking me such a thing. Finally, I responded, "I don't really think that is any of your business."

Imagine our shock in this moment. I mean really! I just could not understand why he would ask such a thing. He had to have been equally shocked that this young lady was being so fresh and talking back so rudely. But he was so kind that he asked me to wait until all who were coming to the Sacrament had finished because he wanted to speak with me about how I was going to confession. The bounty of grace that came from what he shared with me has literally kept me safe in the womb of mother church all these years. He sat next to me in the pew and explained that the Sacrament of Reconciliation is so much more than just taking out our spiritual trash. He lovingly pointed out that the grace we receive in this healing Sacrament is meant to not only purify our soul but give us strength to use the grace in moments of temptation and darkness to avoid the stain of sin. He compared it to the clear, cool water we sip to feel refreshed, but which is also so good for our body.

I thank God for both these priests who were in my life at exactly the right time. As a little girl, my sins were those of a little girl. "I took a quarter off of my daddy's shelf and went and bought fudgesicles." As a teenager, they were becoming more serious; the world around me was a more dangerous place spiritually. The reminder of my stewardship of the gift of grace I had received in baptism was perfectly timed in my life.

Another memory from the time I was an early teen was when I would go horseback riding. I really loved being able to saddle up my beautiful Arabian Quarter horse, Bonnie, and ride through the fields and woods near my home and out to the lake. It was such a freeing feeling, alone with my thoughts and many times my prayers. Please don't get the idea that I was some kind of "holy" kid. I simply liked to talk to God when I was by myself.

I had been taught well, in many regards, by my beautiful Catholic faith, but I thought I was supposed to pray the rote prayers like the Our Father, Hail Mary, Glory Be, and others like them. At that time in my life, I didn't fully understand the deep intimacy our Lord desires with each of us.

So one early spring day, I was riding through the woods, smelling the musky scent of earth as she was beginning to thaw. The new life smells as buds formed on the branches and the songs of the robins as they returned with all the other birds reminded me that winter was over. After the silence of the long winter, the symphony of nature had returned. It was a glorious day to be alive!

As I rode the trails, I heard myself singing. Not just the regular songs that I would sing as I rode, but this time the words were unfamiliar. It was as if a foreign language was coming out of me. Although foreign, it was completely understood in my heart and soul. The melody that accompanied the words was the most beautiful and full sound I had ever heard. It made me want to just stay there in the beauty of God's creation and simply love him. My emotions were all over the place as I knew this experience was holy and yet I felt like I couldn't tell anyone about it. I kept it in but looked forward to my rides and hoped it would happen again.

It did, many times, and each time I felt like I wanted to hear more and hoped to someday figure out what it all meant. My hopes were answered one day when the young ladies' sodality group I belonged to was invited by our bishop from Grand Rapids, Michigan, for a retreat. It was a special retreat in which he invited us to listen to our Lord and hear what the Holy Spirit would share with each of us.

It was the most powerful experience for me to date in my spiritual journey. I learned about how the Holy Spirit fills us with gifts, and I learned that the language in which I had been singing was the language of the Holy Spirit, known as singing in tongues. I treasured this gift that God had given me to sing his praise. I loved singing to him in this way, and whenever it happened, it brought such a true peace and joy. I did not use it in public, but it made me keenly aware that I was never alone, that no matter where I was God was physically with me. Every time I receive the Eucharist, I hear the beautiful words in the language that began when I was so young to come quietly to my lips. Once again, the foundation of my faith was being solidified through this knowledge of his presence and reality, and it would spare my life more than once.

My teen years flew by in a combination of joys and sorrows as many people experience. I really enjoyed school, was actively involved with my horse in 4-H, and loved singing at Mass. I went to Blue Lake Fine Arts camp for music each summer for three years with my flute and voice. I learned to play the guitar, and all these musical talents would come in quite handy when, at the beginning of my senior year of high school, my parents and younger siblings moved to Arizona. I remained in Michigan with my grandmother Julia. Her home was so much a part of my life, and it softened the blow of having a good part of her family moving across the country.

I was voted, along with Jim Keenan (whom you may know as Maynard, the lead singer for the band Tool), as the most talented in my senior class. Ah, music. I stepped up where my grandfather Edward Karas and my mother, Joan Karas Edel, had left off, leading music for Mass at my dear home parish, St.

John Cantius. I was on an early graduation track in high school while at the same time studying solar energy and taking business classes at Ferris State University in Big Rapids, Michigan. My intention was to get a business degree and open my own solar energy company.

Well, small towns are wonderful, and small towns can be something of a pain. Everyone claims to know what everyone else is doing, and before long the gossip mill was going strong and spreading rumors of my dropping out of school, being involved with my boyfriend in very inappropriate behaviors, and drifting away from church—all of which were lies. But my parents, now on the other side of the country, were worried about me, and so I moved to Flagstaff, Arizona, so they could see with their own eyes I was still very much a solid Catholic young woman of faith and morals.

My high school sweetheart, Kurt, was very disappointed, but in just a few months made plans to move to Arizona as well to prove to my family that he was worthy of my hand. Young love is both lovely and ridiculous. With meager funds saved up from his part time job, selling his precious Rickenbacker bass guitar and no plan other than to just get there, across the country he came.

I did graduate high school early but did not finish my engineering degree. Instead we dated, worked, became formally engaged, and planned on September 3, 1983 to get married at the ages of 19 and 20. It seems like God wanted me to keep active in prayer by allowing certain complications to be a constant in my life. He also showed his constant love and care for me by answering prayer just in the nick of time.

Kurt came from a family where each of the men served at least one tour of duty in the military. He felt that if he was going to serve, it would be best if he finished boot camp and basic training before our wedding so that we would not have months of separation once we were married. He joined the army knowing that we would both be open to travel and even opted in his initial paperwork to list Germany as a place he would like to serve.

It was just three days before our wedding when Kurt called me to tell me his leave had been canceled! I was beyond upset. The beautiful day we had been planning was now in danger of being completely ruined. It was crazy.

My mother was having lunch that same afternoon with the governor of Arizona. She explained the situation, and Governor Babbitt called Kurt's army unit to demand this soldier be given the leave that had been approved for his wedding. They allowed his leave for the wedding.

He flew into Phoenix Sky Harbor Airport at 9:30 AM on Friday, September 2. We drove, shall I say, a bit above the posted speed limit to Flagstaff so that we could be at the courthouse before they closed at noon for the long Labor Day weekend. We went running in so that we could get our marriage license, which we had to do together in person during those days! It was crazy!

We had our rehearsal at St. Pius X Catholic Church and a fun rehearsal dinner at La Fonda. I felt like I could breathe again and relax knowing my groom was here and ready to get married.

The next day, at our wedding, the florist came in with all the flowers. They were gorgeous. She asked if I liked my bouquet. I had tears of joy because it was so pretty. She looked relieved and then said that just an hour prior she had come into her shop to get them from the cooler to load into the van, and the front cooler that had my bouquet had somehow frozen the flowers in it along with the bouquet ready for me. It was arranged and fastened to an old lace fan that had been my grandmother's, and she had had only a few minutes to take it apart and get it redone and to the church on time. What a sweet grace it was that it was all okay. The ceremony was one of elegant simplicity, but at the same time an immense portal of grace was being opened up as we celebrated our wedding during Mass. We said our vows to each other, exchanged rings, and then continued with the sacred liturgy to include receiving Jesus in the Eucharist. He became one with us as Kurt and I became one in this powerful Sacrament of matrimony. Another Sacrament, another way for God to show his presence in us, and another source of grace that we were gifted with. We left St. Pius X Catholic Church as Mr. and Mrs. Kurt and Julie Carrick.

Then at our reception, Kurt's Uncle Ray asked me if he could borrow my husband for just a bit. They left and within about half an hour were back. I was puzzled until Kurt and I were in the car after the reception, where I thought we were headed to Phoenix. You see, when Uncle Sam approved him to come home for the wedding, they meant just the wedding. They had only approved the long Labor Day weekend but not the rest of leave that initially had been approved. Our honeymoon was canceled.

When Kurt's uncle learned of this situation, he gave us the incredible gift of the honeymoon suite at Little America Hotel in Flagstaff. Labor Day in Flagstaff, Arizona is always a time when you need to book hotels months in advance. There was no way we were going to be able to have a place for our wedding night there. But somehow Uncle Ray not only gave us the gift of this beautiful hotel, but the honeymoon suite! God sends his angels to us in many a disguise. We did not have to drive to Phoenix after all.

We had Saturday and Sunday together as husband and wife before Kurt had to be back at his unit. He was allowed to have 10 days at home with me a couple of weeks later. I always wondered what became of the couple who originally had the honeymoon suite. I am grateful for the unselfish gift of Uncle Ray and the couple who was willing to give up the suite.

I was excited by the prospect of being a military wife, and the thought of living in a foreign country was very appealing. Traveling was in my blood. When I was a teenager, I had lived in Mexico as an exchange student for three months and as much as I had enjoyed that, I just knew that a life with my husband in a new and exciting place was going to be awesome. He would be going over to get things prepared for us, and the army would send for me in a couple of weeks. I made sure to get everything in order and packed up so I would be ready when my orders would come. This new chapter in my life was going to be amazing!

Chapter 2

Kurt, now in the U.S. Army, and I, now an army wife, moved to Germany. Being so far from the family and friends we had known and in a foreign country was a challenging transition. One of the first trials we faced was that the army sent Kurt there within just a few weeks of our wedding, and I was not able to join him for five months, even though there had been orders for me to do so.

I remember studying our natural family planning course prior to our wedding and thinking, "Now I know they say this is scientific, and my body and temperature and the charts are all saying now is a fertile time. But what is the likelihood of actually conceiving a baby right away?"

Well, our first child was conceived during our few precious honeymoon days. So Kurt's very tiny, slender bride that stood waving at the airport gate five months before was now stepping off a plane with a very round and obviously pregnant belly. He greeted me with such enthusiasm. I was scared to death that he would take one look and freak out. Keep in mind this was way before cell phones, internet, and mommies posting their weekly Facebook photos of the baby bump's weekly progression. Knowing his bride had conceived and seeing her face-to-face after so many months apart was so very different.

God was present in us and in our baby, so the awkwardness was soon nothing more than that nervous feeling that quickly subsided.

***

The first few years of marriage, while in a military community, were really a wonderful blessing. Stationed in Germany, we were blessed beyond blessed to have dear friends who became family. God has constantly shown his love through the dear hearts he has allowed to journey with us: Barb and Howard, Marge and Ken, Fay and Ed, Mike and Cindy, Mel, Margy and Andrew, and Gail.

I believe in my heart of hearts that our precious Lord sent Barbara to me personally. The experience of being a new wife trying to set up an apartment in a foreign country while waiting for literally everything we owned to come over from the States was hard! I had a suitcase and carry-on bag from the plane trip and that was it. We were told it could be months, and it was, before our household belongings would arrive.

My angel-friend Barbara simply showed up and asked what we needed. I almost cried, but instead laughed as I said, "Everything."

She said she would be right back with a "few things." And like a fairy godmother, she returned in what felt like a few minutes with a bed, folding table with chairs, table linens, bed linens, and a set of dishes.

When she realized I was expecting our baby, she even hosted a baby shower for us that was a lovely way to help me get nested and to meet so many wonderful neighbors. She continued to be an angel in our lives in many ways.

***

Just a couple of months later, our sweet baby girl, Edel Marie, was born. She was a few weeks early and was one of the miracles that God gave us. First, she was the very miracle of a human being conceived in her mother.

When I think of each perfect, tiny little cell growing strong and in God's amazing design as each person conceived in the womb grows into the man or woman he has ordained, I am awestruck. I remember sitting in a chair in the living room with my hand on my belly and marveling in the incredible miracle growing within me. I imagined the life of my baby. I could just see her as a little child growing up into a young lady and the full circle of life happening as some day she would be blessed by God to find the man he had designed for her, and they would marry and have a child of their own. All this bounty of perfect love, and she was only the size of my thumb at that point.

My Baby

Refrain: My baby so small inside of me, my baby,
what will you grow up to be?
Will you set the world on fire? Will you be strong? (Refrain)
Will you be happy? Will you smile? (Refrain)
Tell me what you're thinking? What do you see? (Refrain)
Now you're a young lady. Please be good. (Refrain)
You know your man now. You've understood. (Refrain)
Now there's your baby. You've done so good. (Refrain)
Second Refrain: My baby, so small inside of me. My baby,
look what you've grown up to be.

Then there was the incredible grace that she was delivered safely, even though she was three weeks early and the umbilical cord was around her neck!

There was such a powerful moment at her birth that showed me the depth of love that Kurt had for both our precious new daughter and for me. Since she was born early, the doctor did a quick exam. Within two minutes, the OB nurse wrapped her up and walked towards the door. She was taking her to the newborn unit for further care. As the nurse got closer to the door, Kurt had one hand on our child and one hand on me until he could no longer touch both of us. The look in his face spoke volumes. He wanted to stay with me as I was delivering the placenta and then to have the episiotomy stitched up. But our newborn baby girl was moving farther away from both of us.

I told him, "Go with her!" He kissed my face and took off after Edel and her nurse. Such pure love. I know I became a mother as soon as Edel had been conceived, but holding her and being able to look into her tiny face somehow made my motherhood even more real. I was so thankful that our sweet baby girl was with us early in our marriage. She was perfect. She brought such joy and made both Kurt and me feel like we were more a family. The pure joy of loving your infant is beyond words. There is a tender and yet powerful sense of being completely needed by your baby and loving the fact that you love being needed. You want to give them everything possible.

***

Being stationed in Europe, we were able to go to Rome, Assisi, Venice, and Padua to visit wonderful holy sites. God was so generous in giving a young and inexperienced couple some magnificent surprises along the way. One of the most unforgettable trips was to Rome in October 1984. We had purchased our pilgrimage tickets and made sure that our little Edel Marie had the best babysitter on the planet. Our neighbor Marge happened to be a nurse and her husband, Ken, was chief of nurses at the army hospital. They would be watching her for us.

We boarded the bus for the tour of Italy. When we arrived in Rome, our post chaplain, Father John Hart, offered to say Mass at one of the side altars for whomever wanted to come into St. Peter's Basilica. A number of us had gotten off the bus and were headed across the piazza when we heard a voice cry out, "Papa, Papa!"

An ocean of people appeared out of nowhere and pushed toward the doors of St. Peter's. We were literally swept up in the crowd and pushed into the church before the doors closed. The main celebrant was Pope John Paul II. The guest speaker for this culmination Mass of the world priests' retreat was Mother Teresa of Calcutta. I thought we had died and gone to heaven.

With thousands of people in the most beautiful basilica in the world, there was such an intimate presence of Christ among us. I will be 100 years old, gumming my Malt-O-Meal, and I will never forget the sights, the sounds, the smell of incense, and the pure love in the space that day. The prayers were intoned in so many different languages and still they were united as one voice lifting up praise to God Almighty. It was magnificent. It was beautifully and powerfully reminiscent of the language and music I heard when I was a young girl out riding my horse as my soul was introduced to tongues, the language of the Holy Spirit.

It was such a blessing and a gift to my husband and me, who were so young and foolish in such a simple faith that had yet to root deeply. We were good Sunday Catholics. We went to Mass, had our baby girl baptized, had assisted in getting a prayer group started on the army base, and even sang in the choir, but we really hadn't gone deeper yet. God was so patient with us, especially knowing that so much was yet to come.

***

In 1986, the second miracle of our family was born. Even before she was born, our Heidimarie Terese was both infant and teacher. She would teach us that when we pray for a miracle, we should indeed expect one.

A dear priest friend during this same time was Father Clarence Cerwonka. Before I knew I was pregnant, I was having severe abdominal pain and ended up going to the emergency room to be checked out. The physician examined me and promptly ordered an ultrasound. Next, he immediately came in to tell me that I needed emergency surgery to remove an ectopic pregnancy.

The baby had started growing inside the fallopian tube instead of the uterus. I was an emotional mess. I am pro-life! I could not allow a surgery that would remove a baby, even though I knew in my head I was not agreeing to an elective abortion. The baby was growing in the fallopian tube and would not survive, but I couldn't allow the surgery.

I ran out of the hospital and went to my husband's office on the other army post across town. I was crying and talking at once, and his commander told him to take me back to the hospital. As we arrived and were heading in the door, Father Clancy was just walking out. He saw we were clearly upset and asked what was wrong. We explained that I was having an ectopic pregnancy and was struggling about the surgery.

He calmly said, "So what you need right now is a miracle."

I said, "Yes, we do, Father." He began to pray, and I honestly just wanted him to keep praying until the tube would burst on its own and then I could go back in and let them do a quick repair surgery. In my mind, that way I would not be responsible for my baby's death. Again, I was very immature in my thinking and did not understand the teachings of the church about life.

After a few minutes of prayer, the pain had stopped and I told Father that I would go in and let the doctors examine me. When I got back upstairs, the doctor read me the riot act about leaving and asked how I was feeling.

I said the pain had stopped. He looked both surprised and concerned, then immediately had the nurse do another ultrasound.

This time, the tube was perfectly intact, and there was no longer anything in it. In my immature thinking, I was pretty sure God had just removed the baby, but to where? Since the pregnancy test was positive, they did the rest of the ultrasound to include the uterus. Sure enough, there was the exact same size "mass" that had been in my fallopian tube, now safely nestled in my uterus.

The look on the doctor's face was amazing. He just muttered quietly, "This doesn't happen. I am not sure what we were seeing in the tube. Whatever it was is gone. This doesn't just happen." He told me to get set up with my regular doctor for obstetrical visits and let me go home.

During the pregnancy, I had a couple more scares before she was safely born. Carrying her continued to be a blessing, as at one point I was supposed to be flown to Walter Reed Medical Center in Maryland. My physician diagnosed a heart problem for which I was being medicated until surgery could be done, but thanks be to God for going into preterm labor. I was admitted to a German hospital that specialized in women's health and had a great obstetrical wing. They also had a medication that had not yet been approved by the American Medical Association that my American physicians felt I needed in order to safely stop my labor and not cause further complication for my heart issue. The physicians there were able to stop the labor and at the same time find the cause of my fainting spells and heart rhythm issue. I had a potassium deficiency. Thank you, God, and thank you, little baby growing inside of me who brought healing in such a lovely way. When our baby girl was born safe and sound, we celebrated her precious life for so many reasons.

Life with two sweet daughters was such a joy. The tenderness and daily delights they taught us were such a gift from God. Each time we celebrated the joy of baptism and realized how much God loves our daughters, we were a bit overwhelmed.

And we grew in our faith. Seeing Christ afresh in the lives of our children and knowing without Him we would not have had them helped this faith to root deeper and grow stronger.

***

About a year and a half after Heidi was born, I ended up back in the ER. This time, I didn't avoid surgery. I had a large cyst growing inside my ovary, and emergency surgery was necessary to remove it. From a rather young age, I had dealt with endometriosis, and apparently the damage it was causing was not limited to the uterus itself. When I left the hospital after the surgery, it was with the knowledge that there would be no more children since the one ovary was now gone and the tube on the other side was found to be plugged with small, inoperable cysts. We stopped natural family planning and were grateful that we had two beautiful children to raise.

Kurt finished his enlistment term with the army and we did an overseas separation, which meant he got out and we stayed in Germany as civilians. It was a big change once again as we focused on different work but had a lovely opportunity to be able to stay there.

A couple of months had passed. We now had German doctors instead of the army-provided ones. I went in for what felt like strep throat. Imagine my shock when the doctor came in and told me that they would be giving me a safe prescription for the throat issue, which was not strep, since I was pregnant! I asked how, what, when??? I explained that I had been told there would be no more children and since it was normal to miss a couple of cycles after the surgery I had, I was very confused.

He explained that when women are of child-bearing age, they always do a blood test to check for pregnancy before prescriptions are written and mine was positive. I was to-the-moon happy! I got home and told Kurt our news. He was as happy as I was. Being told there would be no more children and here I was pregnant indeed with our third child. It was pure joy to be able to share with our friends and family our incredible news. Such happiness filled our life again.

We were making plans to move to Augsburg, Germany, from Wuerzburg (Unteraltertheim) with Kurt's work and were looking forward to this next chapter and secretly hoping that maybe we would have a little boy this time.

We were just about to the five-and-a-half-month mark when we experienced a devastating blow. I began bleeding and within just a few minutes, our perfectly formed tiny baby boy miscarried. I wrapped him in a little cloth, and we went to the hospital. The nurse took his remains, and the doctor examined me to make sure that everything of the pregnancy had come out. It was complete, and I just cried.

When we were getting ready to leave the hospital, I asked about the baby. They looked confused and said the normal thing was to incinerate the remains. I wept and left with Kurt to go home. I felt empty. I was beyond sad. I felt like I had just left my baby somewhere. There was no funeral. There was no consolation except for a few well-meaning friends who said, "Well, at least you know you can get pregnant, so you should have another baby." Really?

For the first time in my life, I felt like my Catholic faith was letting me down. We are a pro-life church and teach that from the moment of conception until natural death this is a person with a soul, and yet there was nothing to do to acknowledge the life of my first son. I was aggravated by the word *miscarriage*. He was not a miscarriage! He is my baby. We had talked about the name Timmy for him, but now I had nothing but a grainy-looking ultrasound image to remember him by.

Meanwhile, my husband's new career was booming, and the move to Augsburg was to go on as planned. We settled into a lovely house and office space, and day by day, the pain of the loss began to ease. I found peace in the joy of daily life with our daughters.

I also became very good at diabetic care, as in the same time frame our sweet Edel was diagnosed with juvenile diabetes. She scared us half to death when she was diagnosed because she was so young. Her blood sugar level was 682 (normal is 80 to 120). The grace of God was with us as always, though. She was admitted to a German hospital where the standard of care is that the primary caregiver of the child is also admitted. I spent almost eight hours a day learning how to balance insulin doses, being taught all about nutrition and even basic nursing skills like how to give injections and start an IV. It was an amazing 15 days, and when we came home, we knew what we were doing.

God used that incredible gift to help our daughter, and even after we would eventually move back to the United States, he helped others through us. At that time there, was no such thing as carbohydrate counting in the United States. It was all exchanges that had no real scientific value. The German method was exact and kept our sweet Edel healthy. We had once again been directed perfectly by our Lord to be where we should be in order to be well cared for. Once we returned to the United States, we would be called on a number of times to help our family physician with some patients who were more difficult to get under control and even helped a professional ball player's daughter get into the European mode of control before they journeyed overseas. God is just constantly showing his love and protection.

Before we moved back to the States, however, we went through what I would call the dark days of our marriage.

Chapter 3

With my husband's permission, I will share some of what we went through. Once we were settled into our place in Augsburg, Germany, and Kurt was busy with the new work he was doing, we really lost sight of our couple's time.

Coming out of four years in the army, where as an enlisted soldier he was constantly told what to do, there was a newfound pride in each new contract he would make with a client. Selling real estate and money market products was a natural fit for my very outgoing and high-energy husband.

He did so well with the company that he made the top 10 salesman list, and we were given a trip to Venice, Italy. There, the company spent one million dollars on 24 people in a matter of five days. It was like a fairytale. We were flown first class and when we arrived were taken by boat to the Ciga hotel on the isle of Lido. The hotel looked like a castle. Upon arrival, we met our private caretaker. Literally a lady was assigned to us to unpack our bags and touch up our formal wear that was to be different each night for dinner. I felt like a princess.

Those precious days together were, however, a mix of emotions as the sales team meetings took a significant part of each day. We couldn't be together, and the other wives or girlfriends were all about things that I would not participate in. I will just leave it at that. The evenings were such fun though. We had some wonderful dinners, dancing, and couple's time. The pain of losing Timmy was beginning to subside, and the joy of being a couple was returning. It was truly wonderful.

When we got back home to Augsburg and our girls, life was so nice. Being in Germany was a wonderful experience. The culture, the people, and the richness of the history was all around us. We had explored so much of the country with our friends, and it was home for us. The short vacations we had taken over the years living there are some of my fondest memories. Picture it: our Edel and Heidi being photographed over the years with the Alps in the background; dressed up and dancing in their dirndls in front of the various castles of Europe was like picture postcards. Now with Kurt's business continuing to grow and having a home office, we were often hosting clients at our home. He wanted to have someone help me with the girls, so he hired a saint of a woman. I will simply call her Frau Nanny. She was a retired nurse and was completely at ease with Edel's diabetes. She was like a combination of Mary Poppins and a retired German nurse all rolled into one. She would take the girls on walks to the park, and we would shop together.

When Kurt had clients over, I would make delicious dinners. We would wine and dine, and it was again something out of a fairytale. Then the big change of 1988 happened. Much of the U.S. military presence in Germany was no longer needed, and as the troops moved away, so did Kurt's client base.

But he buckled down and worked even harder with the money market company. At one point he was spending so many hours with work and the new assistant he was training that I began to pray God would make it all stop. Our family time became nonexistent.

One day, I asked if we could take some time and go to the park for a picnic like we used to do, and I was delighted when he said yes. We would go tomorrow. I woke up, got the girls ready, and told Frau Nanny to take the day off. When I got downstairs, he handed me a basket that had all the food and drinks in it and said the car was gassed up and ready. Then he helped me put the girls in and turned around to go into the office. I asked him where he was going, and he said he had to work. "Have a nice time with the girls. It will be good to have some quiet in the house." It was a sad day.

He continued working like that until the next big hit. One of the companies he was working with showed that some of their land dealings were less than ethical. Suffice to say, my husband was not going to let the clients suffer, and the only way to get them out of some bad land contracts was for him to pay back his commissions on those deals.

I have never seen a bank account empty out so quickly. We went from not even looking at price tags to trying to figure out how to make it to the next week for groceries. We had to let Frau Nanny go, and I was grateful that we had some time together. It was stressful financially, but Kurt told me not to worry. He said the other company would be the focus now and all would be okay.

Things leveled out for a short time. Then he started working more and more with Katy, the assistant he was training. She was a good friend of mine and a confidant. I was relieved that they could work together, and since her husband was in the army there was still a nice connection to our military community.

Revamping our budget and receiving a small interim loan took the pressure off the finances, but I saw a different look in my husband's eyes. He was going into a dark place and did not want to talk about work. He just kept pushing forward.

I felt the need to go deeper into my faith more than ever before. I could not put a name to it, but it felt like something was coming between us. I started going to daily Mass on base and eventually signed up for a Life in the Spirit Seminar. It was a seven-week course on recognizing and unpacking our spiritual gifts. It felt so good to have that hour of peace at Mass each day and then once a week to gather with a group of other Catholics who also wanted to go deeper.

Four weeks into the study, I was invited to go to the youth conference being held for all the Americans living in Europe. I was pleasantly surprised when Kurt agreed that I should go.

It meant that he would keep the girls, and I would be gone for three days and two nights. But he seemed so lighthearted, and I was excited to be able to go. It was a really nice conference with wonderful speakers, music, and Masses. I felt refreshed at the end of it and knew I wanted to get involved with the parish community back in Augsburg upon my return.

When I got home, though, I was hit with a bombshell. Kurt told me that he wanted a divorce. He and my friend, his assistant, had begun an affair. The betrayal was so deep and so painful I felt like I could not breathe. Pain turned to welled-up anger, and I saw myself smack my husband across the face. I ran to the bathroom to vomit. It felt like there were creatures in my gut trying to get out. Next I ran out of the house and down the block to the apartment of dear friends of ours Margy and Andrew and told them I needed advice and prayer. They were newlyweds that year and they were so kind to invite me in at that hour and help me to calm down. As I explained what Kurt had just told me they promised they would not only pray, but come over to talk with both of us. They were truly offering to be there for us. Once I calmed down I went back to our house to talk to Kurt and try to figure out what was going on between us that was so bad that divorce seemed the only answer.

Behind Kurt's eyes was nothing but darkness. He just reiterated that he was in love with this other woman and that was that. I asked him if Katy had spoken to her husband yet, and he said she was telling him that same night. I wanted to go to their apartment next. I called her and told them that we were coming over. I prayed with such fervor on the way there, literally begging God to protect our marriage and to help us heal what was broken. Her husband was as shocked and pain struck as I was when we arrived and told him what had been going on. I had witnessed people in my life who suffered the pain of infidelity and ended up divorced. Years later, they admitted it was just too hard to face the fact that they didn't know how they could have healed instead. I did not want a divorce. I loved my husband, and I knew in my heart of hearts that he loved me, too. This brokenness could heal if only God would send us another miracle.

The meeting with Katy and her husband felt like an eternity, though in reality it was not very long. But God was with us and when we left to go home, Kurt and Katy had agreed to end the affair and they were both willing to work on their marriages.

It was a strenuous next few months as we went through daily motions of living, if you could even call it that. I protected the girls from knowing anything was wrong by putting on my Happy Mommy face with them and just loving them sweetly. Feeling their love every second of every day was such a gift from God. The love of a child is so tender a gift and so real with no pretenses.

Kurt agreed to give up the sales work and seek regular employment to provide for our family. Unfortunately, he was given some false direction that he had to go stateside in order to apply for the overseas position that was his army specialty. We scraped together the funds to fly him to Detroit to the personnel processing center, only to have him arrive there and find out there was not an opening and in fact they would be closing more of the bases.

I now had to pack our belongings, sell all of the large pieces, and get the house released from the lease without incurring additional charges. Living in a foreign country comes at a price. Everything is scrutinized, and you cannot leave until all has been taken care of. We were there as civilians by this point, and there was no help from the military.

In the midst of the physical work to be done and caring for our daughters alone, I was absolutely overwhelmed. There were moments that I had to remind myself to breathe. I would literally tell myself "Julie, breathe. You can do this. This too shall pass, and you need to care for your baby girls and yourself." By this point, Kurt was feeling horrible about everything, the affair, our hurting marriage, our finances, and now being so far apart. It was torturous. Again, keep in mind this was in 1988. There was no internet at the time. Phone calls were so expensive that we just could not afford to call unless there was a crucial need to discuss something.

What got me through that five weeks was the memory of what we did just before Kurt left for Detroit. We had gone together for the last session of the Life in the Spirit workshop that I had started alone. We sought the Sacrament of Reconciliation, and during the evening prayer time that last night, one of the leaders prayed with us. As she prayed, I heard the beautiful sounds that I had sung to our Lord when I was riding my horse all those years before. It was that strange, yet completely familiar, language that sent a warmth of peace through me. It may seem too simple to say we needed to go to church to begin to heal, but that was exactly what we needed—to be in the physical presence of Christ in the church surrounded by people who want to help others heal and grow in holiness.

I looked over at Kurt and saw the depth of his soul behind his eyes again. The darkness was no longer there. One of the men praying with us asked if we would like an interpretation of the language of tongues that were being spoken and we said yes. He said that what was being spoken about us and by us was, "God would use this couple well in ministry if they would do the ministry together." Also spoken was, "The evil one hates a godly marriage, but that God would protect ours. We need to be obedient to God's desire in our life."

Now with Kurt in the States and me tying up the loose ends in Germany, I fought back the urge to give up by continuing to go to daily Mass before tackling each day's to-do list. When the day finally came to go back to the States, I loaded the girls and our mountain of luggage onto the train that took us to the airport. Looking back at the five years spent in the beauty of Germany, Italy, Switzerland, and Austria, I knew there was so much more good than bad. I knew I had to hang on to that and keep the tenderness in my heart, thanking God for the miracles he had been so generous to give me.

Of course, he had only shown the tip of the iceberg when it comes to how abundant his mercy is and how his sweet Mama Mary would be journeying with us in the years to come. The phrase that I learned and somehow felt the need to hold on to was, "A hardened heart cannot allow my grace to flow, keep your heart soft."

The girls and I landed in Detroit, Michigan, on July 4, 1988. We were back on U.S. soil, and it was time to begin the intense work of rebuilding both our relationship and our temporal day-to-day living.

It was an odd combination of feelings and emotions. I was relieved that our marriage withstood the pain, but moving forward was going to take a lot of work. My heart went out to my husband, who really wanted what was best for us and had worked so hard to make a good life for us. Still, it was hard to trust. I just wanted life to be like it was before the pain. Looking down this new road, I wanted to put the past behind us and look to a future of new possibilities. As hurt and angry as I had been, I longed to be close to Kurt physically again and begin rebuilding our life together. I knew it was going to be a lot of hard work physically, emotionally, and spiritually, and I hoped that God would somehow give us all we would need to begin again. It felt a lot like the day after a thunderstorm. The crashing booming thunder and rain, though loud and fearsome, had its purpose. Now the sun was shining, and it was a new day. After putting on my happy face to visit with some of our Michigan family, the girls and I flew to Utah, where Kurt was waiting for us.

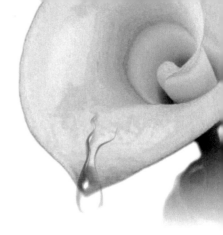

Chapter 4

We made a valiant effort to live in Utah. My brother and his wife were so kind to offer us their furnished basement as a place to rebuild both our relationship and our finances. Kurt and I took positions with temp agencies and were able to put enough away to get back on our feet. But try as we might, we just could not land any permanent positions in Utah.

We both felt that since Arizona was where we married, and it was a growing area, our chances would be good there. We came home to Flagstaff and felt very much accepted in our faith community once again. We both were offered jobs in our respective fields, and life went into a normal routine once again. Work during the week, Mass on the weekends, and we even joined the choir at Nativity of the Blessed Virgin Mary (Nativity BVM) parish. It really felt like we had come home.

There was an announcement one weekend soon after our arrival about a Retorno weekend for married couples, which means literally *a turn around*. The retreat weekend is meant for married couples who need to turn some things around in their marriage. It is a time to pull back away from the world and go deeper into communication with each other and the Lord. It was really one of those miraculous gifts given from our Lord exactly when we needed it most. Up to this point, we were both relieved that our marriage had not taken on the pain of divorce, but we hadn't really looked at what had happened to us in Germany. Honestly, we had been too busy to even think about it, but we didn't want the underlying element to rear its ugly head again. We signed up for the retreat right away.

During the weekend, we learned how to better communicate. We learned some good relationship skills, but most of all we learned that if we were going to be happily married, we needed to have God as the absolute center of our life. We needed Him front and center individually and in us as a couple. God introduced us anew to each other and gave us the gift of a Catholic community of married couples to journey with. It was so lovely to see Mother Mary and Saint Joseph as the model of what we could strive for. Once again, we felt joy flowing back into our life. We also met a dear couple on that retreat, Karen and Dave. They were near our age and both originally from the Midwest as we are. We had an instant connection with them, and as the retreat drew to a close we exchanged contact information and promised we would get together soon for dinner. We became fast friends.

We bought our first house and were feeling strong emotionally and in our marriage. Perhaps it would be the perfect time to see if we could have another child to add to our beautiful family. I went to a specialist to make sure all was okay after having lost Timmy, and with some very simple tests, we were assured all was good to go. Natural family planning, which the Catholic Church asks couples to use in fertility, is such a gift and within two months we were pregnant.

Can I tell you how excited we were? The house was perfect, and with the help of a dear friend from back in Germany, some of our treasures were shipped over to the States with her household goods. She had been storing them for us and shipping a couple of boxes at a time as we would save up for the shipping costs.

The girls were so excited that they were going to have a real baby to play with and love. We were once again in a season of peaceful joy. I was promoted in my federal employment to an administrative position at the United States Geological Survey (USGS) in Flagstaff. Can you hear the sigh of relief right about now?

It was right about this point that I began to write down lyrics and melodies that I would hear in my prayer time. One was the song "Be Still." It was like I could hear the Lord singing it deep down in my heart and soul.

Be Still

When your heart is troubled by the sins that fill this world,
and you cannot feel my joy or peace.
I want you to let your spirit join to me. Rest in me, trust in me and—

Refrain: Be still and know that I am God. Cast your cares
Unto my throne, you'll never be alone.
For you are my precious child, so be still and
Know I am your God.

Don't become so anxious when things don't go
Your way, and you need my guiding hand.
I will give you all things, if you give up your
Concerns, and rest in me, trust in me…and—

When I would go into the beautiful church of the Nativity BVM, I would look at the magnificent painting behind the altar of Saint Anne with the baby Mary on her lap and think to myself, *Oh, little one, what a life you are going to grow up into and live.* Then my hand would go to my own belly, and I would think, *I wonder what you are going to do when you are grown? Your sisters are such a joy, and so will you be.*

We were delighted as a couple to be expecting our baby. Our community was so happy for us. The pregnancy was progressing, and I was already at about the four-month mark. Life was simply good. Just as I had let my heart settle into peaceful, happy days, I felt like the world had once again turned upside down. I felt the same sensation of heaviness in my abdomen, and the blood flow started. Within minutes, our baby had miscarried. Why would God allow this? What possible good was going to come out of this kind of pain again?

I dedicated so many hours and days of my life to protecting babies. I had done sidewalk counseling in front of abortion mills like Planned Parenthood. I prayed for an end to elective abortions. I had been slapped across the face for trying to help a young woman who seemed to be struggling about whether or not to go into the facility one day. I had even been handcuffed and put into the back of a police car once when the director of that abortion facility called and lied about me.

Now here I was holding in my hand once again the remains of my precious, tiny baby. The strongest word I know seems so insignificant when I say I wept. Weeping from the deepest part of my heart helped me to feel a physical release, but the emotional pain was so overpowering.

I went into the house to find Kurt. As he held me, and this time cried with me, I felt strangely as if we were being given a second chance. When we lost Timmy, Kurt did not know how to communicate his feelings and instead he stuffed them inside. Choices he made after that were, in many ways, about trying to deal with something he had no control over. He could not save our son, but he could control other things. That spiral was so unhealthy for him and our marriage.

This time, we turned to each other. We turned together to our Lord. Our community was there for us. Even though a full funeral Mass was not prayed for our baby, we learned the beauty of naming our children publicly and having the Mass of the Angels, where we could hear the word of God, receive the Eucharist, and be reminded that our baby boys are now living in heaven with God and all his angels and saints.

Timmy and Clancy, though both physically present far too briefly in our life, revealed that God knew the short number of their days and that for eternity our saints will be praying for us. It was so beautifully revealed as I went to Mass that next day and looked at the image of Mama Mary that she was with us. I felt like she had led us closer to her Son and each other through Retorno.

This time, instead of going into despair and darkness, we began to ask both of our boys to intercede for us. We got involved with Engaged Encounter Retreats so that we could help couples preparing for marriage avoid some of the pitfalls we had endured.

Shortly after, we were introduced to the life of Saint Benedict, his rule for monastic living, and realized that God was calling us deeper. Kurt and I together did a year of study of the life and rule of Saint Benedict, and at the end we became Benedictine Oblates. We agreed to live our daily life following the ways of this amazing saint.

As lay married people, it was not as life changing as those who would enter convents as nuns or the priesthood, but nonetheless, we would obligate ourselves in living the motto of Prayer and Work insofar as our station in life would allow. It was a great structure of prayer for me and gave me the guidance I felt I was looking for. As oblates of Saint Benedict, we learned and began the practice of praying the Liturgy of the Hours, which is really just praying the prayers of the church at certain times of the day. Knowing that we are praying each day alongside the religious of the faith helped us to feel more connected and accountable for a life of prayer. Knowing that we first need to communicate with God and then each other gives us peace about the decisions we need to make. Then, once we have prayed, we bring our willingness to do the work that God is asking us to do. Priests are required to recite these prayers throughout the day, but as laypeople we offer this sacrifice of prayer as one option for our prayer life.

My favorite daily prayer asking Saint Benedict's intercession is: *Dear Saint Benedict, I thank God for showering you with His grace to love Him above all else and to establish a monastic rule that has helped so many of His children live full and holy lives. Through the cross of Jesus Christ, I ask you to please intercede that God might protect me, my loved ones, my home, property, possessions, and workplace today and always by your holy blessing, that we may never*

*be separated from Jesus, Mary, and the company of all the blessed.
Through your intercession may we be delivered from temptation,
spiritual oppression, physical ills, and disease. Protect us from
drug and alcohol abuse, impurity and immorality, objectionable
companions, and negative attitudes. In Jesus's Name. Amen.*

I was almost afraid to say yes because as I was learning, in order
to go deeper, you have to actually get into the deep end of life.
In order to understand what God was calling me to, I asked my
pastor about spiritual direction and was soon paired with one of
the deacons. He suggested that I attend a Cursillo retreat. Cursillo
is a four-day retreat in which those who attend desire to learn more
about the Catholic faith and how to live it more boldly.

Now, remember the words of the interpretation back in Germany?
"God would use this couple well in ministry if they would do the
ministry together." When married, men are supposed to do the
Cursillo first. Following the men's Cursillo, their wives typically
attend the next women's Cursillo. Since it encourages men to be
the spiritual leaders of the family and home, it makes sense. Kurt
said he was not feeling a call to ministry outside of the Engaged
Encounter with which we were helping. Finally, they made an
exception that I could make my Cursillo. In hindsight, I now
know that I would not have gone out of order. I learned that
after God, my priority is my husband, then my children, then
everything else in life. But being strong willed and trying to go
deeper, I did do the retreat.

My life changed! Coming home after those four days, I knew I
would never be the same. When I went to work on that following

day, it seemed like a year had passed by the end of the day. I just wanted to get home to my husband and daughters and take care of them. Here I was in a dream job with a great salary and benefits, and all I could think about is how I could quit and be a stay-at-home mom. It was crazy to feel such a powerful pull away from the career that was moving in such a good direction that was the answer to prayer when we had returned to Arizona. But I wanted more than anything to start sewing again like I had done in high school home economics class. I wanted to be able to be a classroom mom for Edel and arrange playdates for Heidi and the other little kids of our friends.

Then I started seeing bumper stickers like "stay-at-home moms make a difference" and "homegrown kids are the best." I was freaking out inside with all the mom things I wanted to do. I waited and prayed and prayed and waited for the feelings to go away, but the more I prayed the stronger the feelings got.

I finally told Kurt we needed to talk. I told him that I could not really explain other than I knew God was calling me to live my first vocation as wife and mother at home. We worked through the budget, and with some simple adjustments we knew we could make it work. Plus, I would not be paying for all the costs of going to work like childcare, work clothes, staff lunches out, extra car, et cetera. We agreed that I should quit!

I was so excited to go in and give my notice. Three months and I would be a stay-at-home wife and mother! When I gave my notice to the director, first he laughed and then he said, "Oh, you are serious?" He wanted to know where my promotion was taking me.

Then I laughed and said, "To my home." For the first 30 days, they would not even post my position because they thought I would change my mind. But once the 90 days were done, I was given the lovely last day party at the USGS and sent off with well wishes and the perfunctory "if you come to your senses, you will always have a position here" remarks.

Now, don't get me wrong. I am proud of the work that I did there. It was indeed a good and honorable place to work, and I even got to help one family in particular while working there. One of my employees was pregnant and had developed some major complications and needed complete bedrest for the last three months of her pregnancy. It would have meant using all of her paid leave, going on leave without pay, and then having to come back immediately after the baby was born.

I was able to start a federal employee shared-leave bank so that fellow employees could donate their leave to her account, which allowed her to be fully paid, keep benefits in place, and actually take the 30 days of leave with her baby before returning to work. Of all the work I did in government employ, I think I am most proud of that.

But now on to my kiddos and hubby! It was awesome to be home. I was able to make a real breakfast every morning and sit down to enjoy it. I got to bake homemade cheesy garlic muffins for Edel to take to her Brownie Scout meetings. I was able to watch Heidi in all her creative art projects at the kitchen table. We would go to the park regularly. Then after school we would have snack time and talk about the day. The girls were with me in the kitchen when I would make dinner.

Oh my gosh, I must warn you when you make the decision to make this big of a change, make sure you use a calorie counter daily and ease into it. After my first month at home, I was sure I had developed a thyroid issue and when I sat down with our family doctor to find out why I had gained 15 pounds, he asked me about my new routine. Breakfast at home. Snack. A real sit-down lunch. Snack. Dinner. Snack. Shut up!

But I didn't care. I was so happy I just had to learn balance. Our prayer life as a family was growing, too. Time together allows for such a deeper time of conversation in all ways. Plus, by the weekend I wasn't exhausted to the point of not fully participating in parish life. Kurt and I both started not only singing at Mass but leading the music at Nativity BVM Saturdays and Sundays. It was such a joyous time for us. It was worth the little bit of sacrifice of material stuff in order to really be a family.

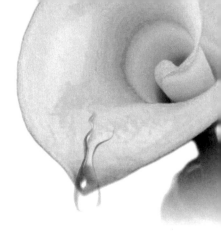

Chapter 5

God is always so faithful as well. He provides in ways we cannot possible plan for when we are simply being obedient. One of our deacons stopped us after Mass one weekend and mentioned the pastor would like to give us a stipend for each Mass at which we led the music. At first, we declined but eventually gave in and thought it a good way to supplement the income I had given up to be home. It was also a way for the pastor and staff to have me directing more choirs, and I was happy to do so.

Our Benedictine community also asked something of us. Oblates are individuals, either laypersons or clergy, normally living in general society, who, while not professed monks or nuns, have individually affiliated themselves with a monastic community of their choice. Our Benedictine community in Flagstaff had roughly 20 members who met to pray and work together on various community projects. We had at this point formally become oblates, and our community was offered the opportunity to have a large house in downtown Flagstaff renovated and available to run as a retreat center. It had been a monastic center and, prior to that, a convent. It was a perfect place. The best scenario was for us to rent out our house and move into the retreat house. It was a win-win for us and for the community.

It was so much fun getting it ready for retreatants. We cleaned, painted, and were able to get all the furnishings needed for a beautiful and comfortable place to retreat from the world. We had the privilege of a chapel that had a tabernacle where our precious Lord was reposed. Kurt continued to work outside the home with his business partners, and then on off days we would tackle renovation projects.

One of the most hilarious of these projects involved redoing the old wood floors in one of the large living rooms. Kurt had rented an orbital sander, but he said it wasn't biting into the wood quite deeply enough. He said it needed a little bit of weight on it. What he meant was he wanted me to sit on it while he moved over every inch of that huge old room. It worked like a charm except that my ears felt funny from all the vibration. Now you have to picture this. I didn't have any earplugs, so I used Kleenex, kind of shoving it in each ear with the length hanging out. It looked like a riot to the people driving up our street and seeing what we were doing through the huge windows that gave them the full show. Still, those floors looked amazing when we were done. Just sayin'.

This brings us into 1992 and the next miracles that our Lord would show us. It was just a few days after the floor refinishing goofiness that I woke up feeling really ill. I wasn't able to kick it for over a week, so I finally went to the doctor. Dr. Mark examined me, asked all the usual questions, and then got more specific. "When was your last cycle?" Being so busy with the new retreat house and honestly just deciding to throw caution to the wind, we had stopped charting. I had to pause and think about it. I figured it had been at least six or seven weeks.

The pregnancy test came back positive. We were pregnant. I was both ecstatic and frightened in the same instant. *Dear God, please let this baby live and be ours to raise and love here on earth.* Then I was totally freaked out by the insane floor sanding escapade! What were we thinking? I went home and told Kurt our news. We were both so happy to be expecting, but almost afraid to get attached to our newest life growing inside of me.

A few weeks later, Kurt came home and found me passed out on the floor in the living room. I was rushed to the hospital, and the nurses did the usual start of IVs and blood drawing. I was examined and told them I was pregnant. They listened with a stethoscope to my abdomen, but the doctor shook his head and said he couldn't hear a heartbeat. I felt numb. I didn't even want to get up when they told me I had to go to the radiology area so they could do the ultrasound. I could not stand the thought of looking at a lifeless baby inside of me. I literally could not bring myself to get up and get out of the bed. I just laid there numb.

Out of compassion for me, the doctor said they could bring in a portable unit. Keep in mind this is 1992. Portable meant a monstrosity of a piece of equipment they had to bring to my room and set up. I didn't care. I just wanted to lie there. The technician came in, and although she was so sweet, I didn't want to hear her voice. That is until she said, "And there is the heartbeat. And there is the spine. And there is the…."

Wait, the what? Heartbeat? I asked her if that meant the baby was still alive. She said, "Yes, your baby is just fine. You are very dehydrated, so it was hard for the doctor to get a good audible of it, but the heartbeat is nice and steady and strong."

I wept for joy. I laughed and cried all at the same time. Then I asked God to please forgive me for my lack of faith. I promised to try to do better in that department, and after being hydrated for a few days and getting my electrolytes balanced, I was able to go home.

My hubby stepped up in a huge way, along with our Benedictine community, as we journeyed through the pregnancy. I did have to take it a bit easier than I had been doing, but regular cooking and cleaning were all just fine to do. I was happy. We continued to sing together for at least one Mass each weekend. In addition, I was directing a couple of other groups.

It was after Mass one Saturday evening that Father Bain stopped Kurt and me and mentioned that he had been approached by the Knights of Malta to give them a list of names of people with serious illnesses. They were going to take a group to Lourdes, France, to the apparition site of our Blessed Mother Mary. He said he had given them our daughter Edel's name.

We asked why. He said he felt he should since she has diabetes. I remember asking him if there weren't other people with more serious life-threatening illnesses who should go. He just repeated that he just felt she should go. It was so funny to think that she would be chosen, but she was.

Just a week later after Mass, he stopped us to say that she had been selected from the list of names given. We were so psyched! Since I was pregnant and trying to stay that way, my mom went as the adult companion invited to Lourdes on a trip of a lifetime. My mother, our daughter, and our niece all flew over together. The two girls had their grandmother with them and thank God she was adventurous.

They spent nearly a week there, attending Mass and going to the famed grotto where Mother Mary has appeared so many times. They really had an incredible time. *48 Hours*, a television news show, was filming stories about miraculous healings and were part of the trip. Upon their arrival home, we were excited to hear how it all went.

There was another young girl Marie who was part of the group. She had an instant, miraculous healing of brain cancer. It was amazing to hear her story. Then there was our Edel. She was convinced she had been healed. She said when she went into the waters, it felt warm like a bath. But the reality was that it was freezing-cold mountain spring water. She said she didn't care what the glucometer said, she knew she was healed.

Right about this point, I was frustrated with God. Why would he have our nine-year-old daughter go halfway around the world on a trip we didn't ask for just to have her come home and still have diabetes? And why was it that Mother Mary would intercede for so many, but not our daughter? It just didn't make sense. It really felt like a mean trick was being played on us. First, we questioned the invitation and made sure a person with a more serious illness had a space available, but Edel was chosen. She went and came back clearly not healed of diabetes. What the heck? It's one little pancreas in the grand scheme of creation! We eventually got over our snit with our Lord and Mother Mary and just chalked it up to a life lesson for some reason.

We continued to serve our Benedictine community, the retreat center, and offer music at Mass. We settled into a good rhythm of life as we awaited the birth of our baby. We had a couple more close calls with this little one, but our daily prayer, Mass, and love and support of the community helped us continue on with the pregnancy.

One of the tender gifts of God's mercy in this pregnancy was that every single morning Father Greg Santos, a Benedictine priest who rented a room in our retreat center, would say Mass. He would knock on the door to our private area and ask me if the "little parasite" and I were ready. There were a few mornings when I was a bit too green at that moment, so he would wait until I was feeling well enough, and then we would have Mass. What an incredible bounty of grace our precious Lord gifted me with.

We were finally in the homestretch of the pregnancy. After preterm labor, medications, and four weeks on complete bed rest,

I was at the 38-week mark. The ultrasound showed all the vital organs looked good, and our fear was over. On Tuesday evening, we stopped the Brethine (terbutaline) and were told that when labor starts to come in and have our baby. Wednesday afternoon, I was in labor.

Our dear, dear friends Karen and Dave were such a beautiful, tender, and powerful testament to what real love and relationship meant during this time. I had asked Karen if she would be there with us for the delivery because nine-year-old Edel wanted to be present as well. To show the depth of trust and love in our friendship, you need to know that Karen and Dave were unable to have children. Infertility was a sad burden they had endured for years. To know this and still appreciate that they were the only people we wanted there with us at such a powerful moment shows both our love for them and the trust we had that our friendship was able to handle it.

Since we could only bring one person in with us to assist with Edel while Kurt was busy as my coach, we asked Karen to plan on being there. She and Dave both agreed that in case, for some reason, she couldn't get there in time, he would bring Edel in and watch over her during the birthing process. Unfortunately, when the day came, Karen couldn't get there in time. It was absolutely maddening. I once again wondered why God would put the thought in my mind and heart to trust our friendship enough to ask her to be there and then not let her get there in time.

But our sweet little Paul was born that beautiful, sunny November afternoon healthy and safe. I was overjoyed. God had allowed us to keep him here to raise. Literally minutes later, Karen came in and we hugged each other and the new little man. We spent that day together in the hospital marveling at this new precious life and the absolute wonder of God's creative love. Of course, we asked them to be his godparents and they said yes.

The next day, Karen and Dave brought letters they had written to us and Paul so someday we could share what impact the day had been to all of us. What they shared with us was beyond beautiful; it was a lovely blessing. Being unable to have a baby up to this point, Karen had opened to the idea of adoption, while Dave shared that he didn't know if he could love another's child as his own. Witnessing Paul's birth opened his heart to see the knowledge of what was already there; yes, he could indeed love a child completely as his own, even if he or she was born of someone else physically.

This tiny person had shown the four adults in the room how precious love of another is. Biology was not what makes us love each other. It was a friendship rooted in the pure love of God, who had brought us all together years prior when we met on that beautiful Retorno retreat. Coincidence? Absolutely not.

What we would all learn soon enough was that their precious daughter had already been conceived and was growing strong and well in her birth mother's womb. They would become a family of three in July.

We cared for those who came for retreat until the following August, and with a newborn baby it was kind of like having our own version of the family circus. With Edel and Heidi busy with school right next door to the retreat house, we were kind of growing up in the public eye. We had served the community well, but we were open to God's will when Kurt's work offered an opportunity to spend some time in Pennsylvania and Michigan. He has been working as a consultant for a medical products firm and had developed a surgical equipment suite for surgical ophthalmologists. There was a group in Pennsylvania that wanted to form a larger partnership, and it was one of those times we chose together as a couple to move for a career advancement. We talked it over with the girls, who were now seven and nine years old. They, of course, had made friends in our Flagstaff community, but honestly seemed open to a new place on the other side of the country. Being born in Germany and having traveled so much in their short lives, they were part gypsy I think. We would, of course, have to let go of the retreat house and figure out who should be the next live-in caretakers. Our community prayed about the decision and then asked my parents, who by this time had also become Benedictine Oblates, to come in as caretakers of the retreat center. They agreed, and we said goodbye to Flagstaff for a while. Sometimes moving away from the familiar can be a time of enlightenment. We settled into a rented home in Paoli, Pennsylvania, and planned to be there for as long as it would take to get the new partnership up and running smoothly. After three months, Kurt was becoming really frustrated with the "partners." They were trying to take over the product line he had worked so hard to develop, and it was clear that he needed to end the negotiations of the partnership. By now, we were beginning to learn that if God would have us move to Pennsylvania, there must be a good reason. It was a very expensive place to live and when we looked at a map trying to decide what we were being called to next, we both felt like Michigan was where we should be going. We had not thought initially to move to Michigan, but it seemed like God was bringing us there via Pennsylvania. It was a short move and to a very low cost of living town that we were both so familiar with, having grown up there. Back in Manistee, where I had been born and near to both of our families, it was a great place to once again regroup. This time, however, it was planned together. In a funny way, it healed and closed the chapter of our life that had been so broken back in 1988. A beautiful gift that we received as a family while living in Manistee was that I was able to visit my 94-year-old grandmother daily. She was the grandma I lived with when my family moved to Arizona back in 1981. We would have loved to have stayed in Michigan, but the winter was not kind to our daughter Heidi. She just could not stand the cold damp weather. It sounded like we had a baby seal living with us at nighttime as she caught the croup. We made the decision to return to Flagstaff in the early spring, but there was great purpose for both Kurt's work and my calling from God to have had this time away from the busy life in Flagstaff.

During the months away, I began to write more and more lyrics and melodies. The songs seemed to write themselves. I could hear the tender description of Karen's story of motherhood as she shared how their daughter grew in her heart as she developed in her birth mother's womb. I recalled how my sister Lori spoke with such deep longing and love of her daughter whom she had placed for adoption so many years prior.

These two women, whom I love so much, taught me in their desire for real life, what unselfish love means. To give and receive the gift of life in the way each of them did was truly heroic. Their two daughters are their treasures. When I pondered what their hearts must have felt, it came out as the song "Kateri."

Knowing that the birth father of my sister's child was Native American, I was intrigued to learn more about Saint Kateri. She, too, was a heroic woman. She was a Native American who became Christian and was ultimately martyred because of her Christianity. Those of us close to Lori asked daily for Saint Kateri to intercede on behalf of her daughter. It seemed the most natural thing to refer to her as Kateri.

When I would play the song, the lyric and melody would bring such strong emotion out of me. I felt that if it could be shared, maybe lives would be touched to open to the gift of life through adoption. I didn't know why I was writing songs at that point in my life. It just seemed like the experiences of those around me, whom I loved so much, needed to be written down. The music just came out of me. I always wondered when the day would come that Lori would see her daughter again.

Kateri

God, you gave to me the very best you had to give,
You gave to me a child destined to live.
This gift of yours to me, was not for me alone.
I was simply chosen to give her a home.

Refrain: Thank you for the strength you gave me
When my life was crashing down around me.
Your spirit made me strong enough to choose
The gift of life. Baby mine, alive and dear, sweet Kateri.

Choices I had made that brought her to conception
Are not the ones that lead me to your divine perfection,
Through her life, her very existence, prove to me, my God's sweet
persistence. And lead me on my daily way where Jesus heals and I
can pray.

Your life and mine are intertwined now,
Kateri's Life we always share somehow.
Though her mom is someone else now, my heart is truly aware,
of the gift, the precious child I carried,
in my womb while in your heart.
Her smile will fill your life with laughter, and
Take the pain from my own.

We gave Michigan our best shot, but after careful discernment we knew we were being called back home to Arizona. We were both grateful for the time spent there and being able to have such precious time with our extended family members. Sometimes distance can strain family relationships, but we were blessed with this time to realize we may have physical miles between us and them, but in our hearts and prayers they were never more than a thought away. The move to Arizona back in 1982 was quick. The move from Germany back to the United States was quick. With this move, we took time to plan together as a couple and ask God what he wanted for us. Even though it was a double move to Pennsylvania, Michigan, and back to Arizona, it was a healing gift from God that allowed us to find closure in a number of ways.

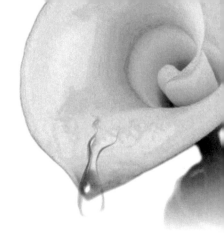

Chapter 6

In May 1994, we moved back to Flagstaff, and I was asked to pick up where I had left off with leading music in the Nativity BVM parish. After a few months, Deacon Bill approached me and asked me when I was going to do what I was being asked. When I asked him to explain what he meant, he said I could either listen to the people asking for my recorded music or perhaps the good Lord needed to knock me upside the head to get my attention. I honestly did not realize how many people asked me for music until he brought it to my attention.

After that day, I realized that literally every single time I sang in public someone would ask me for my music. So Kurt and I thought we should make a record. We went into a local garage studio along with my sister Patricia, who played piano so beautifully, and we recorded a Christmas project entitled *December Road*. Kurt and I played guitar, Patty played piano, and I sang my little heart out.

I think we took a couple of takes on each song, had Art, the studio owner, mix it for us, and we had it ready to send off to a manufacturing company back east. It is hilarious to look back on, as I can still see the 18-inch dragon lamp with blinking red eyes glowing through the window while I was singing sweet Baby Jesus songs from my heart.

I felt so high tech when I took a photograph of the most beautiful, snow-covered landscape that Kurt shot when we lived in Germany and a picture of me dressed up for the cold to a local shop to have it photoshopped. That was super high tech in 1994.

Our order of CDs and cassette tapes (that cracks me up to even write!) came in, and I was so excited. But now what the heck was I supposed to do with these? We had 500 of each. Our parishioners soon bought those, and I had to order more. Then I did a women's conference for the Four Corners, and I had to order more. It was crazy. People were buying this Christmas project before, during, and after Christmas. We ended up selling over 3,000 copies in three months.

I was shocked to say the least, and I asked my husband what we should do since it seemed God was calling us to a music ministry. Kurt had a career change upon our return to Arizona as he accepted a position with the Arizona Department of Public Safety. He wanted a more stable income and health benefits package for us, and his work for the Highway Patrol Division would allow him to use his degree and management skills well. He said he would support what I felt God was calling me to do, but he said he was not hearing it for himself. When people ask me how and why I became a recording artist and inspirational speaker, I simply say God asked me to be obedient. I tried to be obedient, and I am living proof that God will supply all that is necessary if we are open to his desire for our life. "December Road" is such a lovely proof of this grace.

December Road

Mary and Joseph traveled long ago to the town of Bethlehem, many miles away. Carrying a baby warm within her womb, she wondered what would happen; His birth was coming soon. Many miles away from home, strangers they would meet, but resting in the plan of God, her heart was filled with peace.

Refrain: December Road, see it covered with the snow. Feel the wind now as it blows. There is wonder as we walk to the place where it will lead. What does Jesus have in store for those who travel down December Road.

Overhead, a brilliant light has filled the sky, a star that led three wise men in search of their King. They followed it untiring right to the cave and brought with them their treasures to lay before their King. They entered the stable door to see the King they had waited for and upon their bended knee, gave their gifts to Him.

Realizing now it's been two thousand years, makes me stop and wonder, "What can we do for Him?" How can we give a gift that's fit for Him, our mighty Savior, the One that we adore? We can give to Him our lives, let Him fill us with desire, and give us all the strength we need to travel down our road with Him.

I began to listen to other Christian artists who had professionally recorded projects available to review, and I knew I had to step it up if this was going to be a real thing. And the more I prayed about it and learned about costs, I just couldn't see how it could happen. God knew how it would happen.

I received a call from a music scout in Nashville, Tennessee, by the name of Robert Metzger, who asked me to come for the *Star Search* talent show. Being somewhat skeptical of anything like that, I needed details. He said if the music was good enough and if my talent was of a high enough quality, then a sponsor would pay for the trip and the initial recording. After that, we would see whether a record deal would be in the cards.

I was shocked when the local Pepsi company sponsored me! I mean seriously. It was thousands of dollars, and the next thing I knew I was on my way to Nashville. I sang for *Star Search*. Robert Metzger, who arranged it, met me as promised, and we went into the studio to record five of my songs. I sat in Tom T. Hall's artist's chair at Chelsea Studio and hoped I didn't look as terrified as I felt. These people were professional studio musicians who had played on so many recording artists' records, and they were going to hear my music and record it. I felt so out of place.

Then the session started. Tony Migliore, the producer, handed out charts to the players, Gary Lunn (remember this name), Bobbi All, Jerry Kroon, John Willis, Lori Brooks, Rick Gibson, and Doug Clemmens. They listened to my simple guitar playing and singing with such tender patience. Then they played what they were feeling from my description of it, and the background vocalists sang harmonies to my songs.

I started crying. I could not believe how beautiful they made my simple songs sound. It would have been so easy to give in right then and there and do what Robert wanted me to do. He asked me to "soften" the Jesus focus a little bit. He said, "There is no need to actually say his name. You can just allude to him and people will get it."

When he listened to the first take of the track, he asked me if he could give it a little more of a country feel. I told him I was not comfortable singing country music. We had discussed Christian music and that was what Pepsi had sponsored me to do. We finished the five songs. I was given a wonderful tour of Nashville, and after a few days, I was on my way home to Flagstaff. I had a five-song demo and a Christmas record to my name.

A few months later, I returned to Nashville to receive three awards from the Academy of Independent Recording Artists. They gave me the honors of Horizon Artist of the Year, Female Vocalist of the Year, and Single of the Year. Tony Migliore had submitted my recordings as soon as I had recorded them and later told me that out of all the artists brought through, he felt I had the most potential and integrity.

I came home and told the Lord I would do what he wanted, but I needed his direction. I asked him to send someone who could direct me in recording professional-quality music, but who would keep the authentic integrity of the message intact.

God answers prayers. Again, on a Saturday evening in the beautiful church in downtown Flagstaff, a man came up to me at the end of Mass and asked me if I truly believed what was spoken about in the Catholic service. I asked him what part of the Mass he was referring to, and he said, "Communion." He asked if I truly believed that the bread and wine become the body and blood of Christ. I told him that I believe with every fiber of my being that I receive Christ in what looks like bread and tastes like wine but is no longer those but him.

We chatted for almost half an hour before he left. I thought he looked familiar. It was a couple of weeks later, when he came to Mass again, that I recognized who he was. He was dressed simply in jeans, a rather dingy T-shirt, and sandals. Kurt and I sang "Sometimes By Step" written and recorded by Rich Mullins after Communion. The man asked a few more wonderful questions about the liturgical celebration of the Mass, and once again we spent about half an hour chatting.

Just before he turned to leave, he said, "By the way, I really like the song you sang after Communion." That was when I realized it was Rich Mullins I had been chatting with. We exchanged contact information; he was so open and honest about the recording industry. He told me what was good about it and what to avoid to keep personal and spiritual integrity. There was such a powerful lure for fame and fortune that affected so many people so badly.

To call him a close friend would be an overstatement, but as colleagues we were able to share a lot. He would call or stop in to ask questions about the Catholic faith that I answered from my personal experiences as a cradle Catholic. I would ask questions about the contemporary Christian music industry and community, and he was very forthcoming about ways to proceed with caution and the best ways to make sure I was getting the best quality of musicians for recordings while keeping my own identity and integrity in my music as a Catholic. He told me about the Gospel Music Association and said it was a good way to learn more and of course do some networking.

Shortly after we had begun communicating, I received a phone call from the Catholic artist John Michael Talbot. He was interested in starting a group specifically for Catholic artists and invited Kurt and me to come to his place in Arkansas for the initial meeting. It was a great idea, and for the first few years I was happily a member of CAM (Catholic Association of Musicians). I loved the idea that there could be a group of likeminded folks who could assist in accountability of both the quality of music being produced and the faithfulness of belonging in the Catholic church.

At the same time, I was also a member of the Gospel Music Association. They had been in place for a very long time, and the way people took seriously the duty of writing, recording, and presenting beautiful music to honor God was marvelous. I felt like I really had the best of both worlds. One of the main reasons I didn't stay with CAM beyond the first few years was that I felt that it lacked the tough love needed to help people truly discern their calling. Wanting to be a recording artist and being one are two different things. There are writers, composers, singers, administrative support roles, and many other components to the industry. Too many times people miss the part they are gifted for.

I had taken on more events regionally and even a few dates in other parts of the country to the point that the trip to the Phoenix airport was getting to be a bit tiresome. The tiny regional one in Flagstaff had so few daily flights and most of them had me fly to Phoenix, where I would sit and wait for hours for connections to cities around the country. Never was there a non-stop itinerary. One such trip was planned for Illinois to do a concert with Rich. He asked me if I would open the concert. I was excited to do this, especially with the Ragamuffins, his band, whose members I had had the pleasure of meeting in Nashville.

I loved the honesty I found in him, and the real and raw way he shared his love for Christ. He was teaching me that there is no need for a gimmick or stage persona. All I had to do was be myself and share my stories of life with Christ through my witness and music. It would be the first time that I opened for another artist, not to mention one of his caliber.

It was a week out from that date when a rather strange occurrence happened. It was September 20, 1997, right at the end of the Saturday evening Mass at Nativity BVM when I looked at the back of the church and there was Rich again. He didn't come up to chat this time, he just waived and headed out the door. I was speaking with a few other folks who had come to say thank you for the music, so I didn't get a chance to go talk with him.

After we finished putting the instruments away, we went to the house to pick up our kiddos, who were with my mom. When we walked in, I mentioned to my mom that I wished she had come to Mass since Rich had come by again and I would have liked to introduce them. She looked at me in a strange way and said, "You could not have seen him tonight. We had a call while you were at Mass from his people to tell you that he was killed in a car accident yesterday."

Words failed me in that moment. It was so sad to learn of his passing, and to this day I often think of that image of him waving and heading out the door of the church. There are some things that just cannot be explained.

***

I know that God has given me the gift of music. I know that he has placed it in my heart to share this music and the prayer that goes with it. I must admit it was nice to receive compliments when people were touched by different things that I would sing. The Lord knew that I needed a good dose of humility, however, before the ministry would go anywhere.

Our daughter Edel was going to Gallup, New Mexico, to work with a group of Mother Teresa's nuns for her spring break. The trip was set and a number of young ladies from St. Mary's Catholic School in Flagstaff were ready to go. Just a day before the trip, one of the chaperones had to cancel. Without the right number of chaperones, the trip would be canceled. So Edel asked if I would go and ensure that they would be able to do their spring break community service hours.

I was happy to go. I was actually prideful when we arrived and Sister Margaret, the mother superior at the community, welcomed us and said she was so honored that I was there. She said that perhaps during our visit I would perform some music for them. I said of course, that I would love to. We were each shown to our rooms and given our various assignments for the week.

My first assignment was in the kitchen. I was standing next to Sister Beatrice, a sweet little nun no more than four feet eleven inches tall. She had the most beautiful and almost at the same time the most infuriating smile I've ever seen. She and I were supposed to take care of the fruits and vegetables for those first two days. That meant huge crates five by five by four feet tall of produce were brought into this large industrial kitchen. Next to the crates were countertops with little plastic containers, lids, rubber gloves, and paring knives.

We were each given a paring knife and as many pairs of gloves as we needed to get the job done. Our job was to rinse and then trim each vegetable and fruit and put them into plastic containers. Strawberries, tomatoes, cucumbers, onions, you name it; they were all in these giant crates. They were only separated in layers by large leaves of lettuce. Halfway through the first morning, I was really aggravated. I went to Sister Margaret and asked her where on God's green earth they were getting their produce from. It was half rotten, and they needed a different supplier. She smiled at me and said the produce was donated. And it was not half rotten, it was half good.

I felt like I had shrunk down to about four feet eleven inches tall myself. I went back into the kitchen with Sister Beatrice and continued trimming vegetables and fruits. I continued to watch her smile, and little by little I stopped feeling aggravated and infuriated. Instead, I needed to know the answer to a question. I asked her how she was able to smile and find such joy while preparing food that would otherwise be discarded and turn it into beautiful meals for hungry people.

She said her joy came from the fact that every time she moved her paring knife through a piece of fruit or vegetable, she could see that it would become nourishment for someone. And not nourishment for just anyone, but nourishment for Christ himself. She saw Christ in each of the homeless people who came to the soup suppers. She saw Christ in every one of the Native American people who lived on the reservation where they would deliver meals daily. She saw Christ in the elderly who lived in the nursing home on the other side of the campus, and the meals that were prepared for them fed Christ as well.

I was amazed at this woman. I began to realize the need to find gratitude in my heart—to find grace in every moment of every day and to be thankful to God for it. She was a living testament to grace.

On the third day of our time there, Sister Margaret came into the living room with a guitar. I was so excited! I would finally get to sing some music and use what I thought was my best talent for this community. Instead, however, as I looked at the guitar, I realized the strings were so old, oxidized, and brittle that there was absolutely no life left in them at all. They needed to be changed. When I mentioned this to Sister Margaret, she said she hoped that I would be able to restring the guitar and have it ready to play.

I ran out to the music store in town, bought some guitar strings, came back, cleaned, and restrung the guitar. It was a lovely old

Yamaha that sounded beautiful once it had fresh strings. As I finished tuning it and as I was getting ready to play my first song on it, Sister Margaret said, "Thank you so much" and then took the guitar and gave it to one of the other little nuns who was sitting there. She played a couple of songs, and the community sang. Then it was time to go in for supper.

The next morning, I was back in the kitchen with Sister Beatrice. This time, two giant crates of potatoes were brought into the kitchen. I had to laugh as I thought to myself, *there is not going to be any singing on this trip but lots and lots of cooking.* Sister Beatrice and I spent the entire day peeling potatoes, washing potatoes, cooking potatoes, and making scalloped potatoes. We made giant pots of potato soup.

At the end of the day, when everything had been prepped and chilled and some things frozen for future use, we all went into the chapel. This was our final night there in Gallup with the sweet sisters. After Communion, Sister Margaret asked me if I would sing a song for the community. My hands were tired from the work in the kitchen, but I had never felt more joy than I did at that moment to sing for the community.

I sang "Be Still." I think the words of that song, inspired from Psalm 46:10, resonated deeper in me than they ever had before. Every gift that I have is a gift from God. Every comfort that I have is a gift from God. Realizing that every movement, every breath, every grace that I have in my life is a gift from God is the treasure that I brought home with me from that trip to Gallup. I will be ever grateful to Sister Beatrice and Sister Margaret for the lovely gift of humility that blossomed into such grace for me.

Just before we got into the van to head home to Flagstaff, Sister Margaret asked me to come into the kitchen for just a minute. I went in and there in one of the large pantries was a great big box. She said it had arrived the week before, and they didn't know what it was or how to use it. It was a mechanized industrial potato peeler! How our Lord must have been laughing along with us.

When we arrived back home to Flagstaff, I took our dirty clothes out of the suitcases to wash. I opened the lid to the washing machine and thanked God for the time in which we live. There is such luxury in a machine where all I have to do is put my clothing in, add soap, and push a button and my laundry is washed for me. To simply put it into a machine right next to it where it is dried and even fluffed so that there are few wrinkles is a blessing.

I had been taking these for granted my entire life until I spent time learning real grace. I honestly mean it when I say I never take for granted anymore the simple machines for laundry or dishes. They would become a source of Thanksgiving grace in my daily life.

That same week, I received a call from a lady in our parish. She had a piano that she wanted to give away. Since I didn't play piano, I told her that I would check around with the families in our neighborhood to find out who would put it to best use. After checking with all the neighbors with kids and anyone who might have an interest in learning piano, I did not have any takers. I called her back and said I was sorry that I could not find a home for that beautiful instrument. Then she explained that what she was initially trying to do when she called was give it to me. I was delighted to accept the gift, and I thought that maybe someday I would learn how to play it.

Within about a month, my sister Patricia, who had played on the *December Road* CD, moved to Pennsylvania. The other two piano players who regularly played at my local and regional events also moved to different parts of the country. I remember distinctly one Tuesday morning walking into the living room and looking at the piano. I knew where middle C was on the instrument. I sat down and figured out the notes that made a C chord. Then I did the same with each of the other chords much like playing the guitar. I am not kidding when I say that within about 35 minutes, I was playing piano.

What's funny about this whole thing is that I love the piano, but I have the attention span of a gnat when it comes to sitting down and actually learning an instrument. I always thought it would be beautiful to be able to accompany myself singing with piano and once had even mentioned to God that if he wanted me to play, he would have to help me.

The telephone rang and our daughter Edel answered the phone. It was Kurt calling from work to check in on everyone. When he heard the piano playing in the background, he asked Edel who was at the house visiting. She said no one. He asked her who was playing the piano and she replied that it was mom. He said she doesn't play the piano. And Edel replied, well she does now.

The next weekend when we went to Mass at Nativity BVM, Father Dan, who had suggested to me that I should learn how to play the piano, was shocked when I sat down and accompanied Kurt on guitar. Again, what a lovely grace.

Chapter 7

January 1, 1998, Kurt and I decided to begin the new year with a nine-day novena to the Holy Spirit. A novena is a simple but very focused prayer that is prayed for nine consecutive days, weeks, or months. We wanted to surrender to whatever God wanted us to do in the coming year.

In February, I received a call from a Catholic priest friend who was asking for music for a couple of my songs. He wanted his choirs to learn them and wanted the sheet music and recordings of them. We had not seen each other since he was a pastor up in northern Arizona, so we made a date to come down to the Phoenix Valley to see him and bring him the music in person. I had done a simple recording at our house and dutifully put it on a cassette tape. Just before we arrived at the parish, I popped it into the car stereo to listen and the tape was somehow now blank. I was a bit embarrassed when we met with Father Larry and asked if he had a way for us to record in the church. They did, so we went in, and I sat down at the piano to record it. Within just a few minutes, much of the staff had come in to see what was going on and listen to the music.

As I finished recording, the pastoral associate invited herself to join us for lunch. Before we left to head back to Flagstaff, she and Father Larry offered me a position to be the new director of contemporary music at St. Joan of Arc. I told them we would pray about it, but that honestly it was just not feasible for us to move down to the Valley. The salary was great, but not enough to offset Kurt's primary income with the Arizona Department of Public Safety. The thought of being close to a major airport was tempting, but we headed north and put thoughts of the Valley behind us.

The next day, Kurt asked me to pray one more novena to ask our Lord for a definite answer with regard to the possibility of moving. It was on the second day that there was a terrible accident on I-40 in Flagstaff. The highway patrol was almost overwhelmed by the number of vehicles involved. Kurt was in the dispatch center in the middle of the action with accident scene emergency management.

Once it was all finally under control, he asked one of the supervisors what the protocol was for someone interested in a transfer to headquarters in Phoenix. He was told he would have to write a letter to the director, but transfers were scarce. He sat down and wrote the letter. It was only five o'clock in the morning when the director unexpectedly came into the dispatch center. Kurt laughed and told her that she had saved him a stamp as he handed her the letter. When she realized what it was about, she immediately offered him the transfer and even offered to take care of the move if he was serious about it.

He called me and said we had our answer about the move to the Valley. I called Father Larry and said if he could wait until June 1, then I would accept the position. He and the staff were delighted that I was willing to come and take on the job of directing and further developing a contemporary music department at the parish. They had wonderfully talented people in place for both traditional and contemporary music, but they really wanted me to be part of the staff. I made it very clear that I would be continuing to build the ministry that I knew God had called me to, which meant I would be gone a couple of weekends each month.

The beauty of developing the large group of volunteers to work together was that I could plan the liturgical music, prepare it, and have everyone rehearsed, so that whether I was there or not, the music for Mass would be engaging and beautiful. Once again, it was our Lord who gently moved me into the direction of a national ministry but did it in a way that was possible for me to keep the proper order of my vocation: first wife and mother, then an artist using her gifts to teach the beauty of the faith.

It was with mixed emotions that we made the move to Scottsdale, Arizona, from Flagstaff. We knew it was right. We were responding to what we felt was God's calling, but it was hard to leave family and friends. Nativity BVM Parish, St. Pius X, where we had been married in 1983, and now the combined community of San Francisco de Asis was such a huge part of our life. We experienced such healing grace and love there. Such beautiful gifts were given to us over the years, like Edel's trip to Lourdes, the beginning of the ministry, to say nothing of the dear friends and family.

We'd just finished renovating a house we bought. I'd always wanted a big bay window—the kind with a comfortable cushion and lots of cute little pillows that I could relax in as I gazed outside. While the final coat of wood sealer and protectant was drying on my new bay window, the moving truck was pulling up out front. Now that we were re-locating to Scottsdale, we decided to rent out our home. Our tenants would thoroughly love my beautiful bay window. It is funny how God has taught the lesson of detachment from worldly things.

We pulled up to our new house in Scottsdale on June 1. The kids were so excited because it had a pool, and they could already feel the heat. Paul, now five years old, was so funny! He stood at the edge of the pool, rubbed his hands together and said, "Mommy, I can't wait until winter!" I asked him why and he said, "'Cause when this pool freezes, it is going to be great to ice skate on!"

Oh, sweet child! Edel was anxious, but at the same time excited to be going to Horizon High School because they had a great volleyball team. She was going to be at summer camp to get ready for tryouts. Heidi would be at Sunrise Middle School playing basketball. The girls, though nervous about moving from a small Catholic school in Flagstaff to huge Class A public schools, were psyched.

We were settling in well when we had the most amazing gift and shock all at once. Edel went to day camp for volleyball for a week and by the end of it was pretty sore. She also needed to have her sports physical for the new school. We scheduled her with our new family physician. She told him that it was her knees and lower legs that seemed to be most painful after a big workout.

He ordered x-rays of her knees. While we were still in the radiology department, the tech came out to tell us that they would also need to do an MRI of her legs. They did the imaging study and said our doctor would go over the results with us.

A couple of days later, we went in to see the doctor. He asked to speak to Kurt and me first. He told us that he normally expects parents to give the full medical history of minor patients. I was wondering why he was being so direct with us. I had filled out her paperwork and was very clear about her diabetes.

He asked us, "When was her last treatment for the bone cancer?" What? Bone cancer?! I felt sick for a second.

I asked him, "What did you find in the MRI? Does our daughter have cancer?"

He could see the shock on our faces so he said, "Not now, but these…" he put the films up on the light bar, "these are the post-treated, encapsulated tumors, or scars if you will, from when she had bone cancer. This is what they look like after successful treatments."

Kurt and I looked at each other and both said, "Lourdes" at the same time. Once again, Mama Mary had interceded for us. We were complaining that she didn't get the healing of diabetes back in 1992, but she knew what our daughter needed much more than we did. Our precious Lord revealed this healing six years after the fact as we sat with this physician.

After we composed ourselves and our daughter was brought in, we talked about the reality of how to proceed if she was going to be serious about professional sports someday. With the areas of weakness in the legs, they spoke about the possibility of surgically breaking her legs to add a cross section of calcium where they would heal. She definitely did *not* want to do that. Instead, she found her true passion in music. She joined the choir and loved it.

I began my work at St. Joan of Arc Church. I loved being able to direct larger choirs and bring out the talents of individuals. I knew that it would be a lot of work to balance my commitments, but these folks had great talent and they brought their best. It was good that there were natural leaders in each group so that when I left to do my concert ministry on the weekends, there would still be music at Mass.

I remained a member of the Gospel Music Association and during one of the "work" weeks with the GMA in Nashville, I was introduced to Lana from the Gaither Resource Center. It was one of the places Rich Mullins spoke highly about. We hit it off so well that I knew I'd found the perfect place to record my first serious project. Since I had the five songs nearly complete from my first trip to Tennessee and I had been writing and preparing new pieces to add to it, it was the perfect time to dig deeper and see what more our Lord would have me do with this music and witness of the faith. It was finally time for a full record, and it just felt right to have it focused on the theme "Child of God."

The song "Kateri" ended up as the title track, and the rest of the songs were filled with so much of my heart and love. The session players hired by my producer, Mark, were talented and extremely open to making sure the music was just perfect. After a week of working long hours, my recording was done. The musicians, the background vocalists, the engineers, and the art design people made me feel like I really belonged there. They encouraged me to use this new project to make a difference for people questioning the life of the child in the womb.

They said it also felt like a project that could help each and every one of us look at the gift of our free will. How would we use it? Of course, one of the songs that was recorded on there is titled "Free Will." I had been at a writing course with Cindy Morgan, an artist whom I really respect, in Colorado. It was sponsored by the Gospel Music Association, and I had the privilege of singing a number of my original songs in between Cindy's presentations.

I was in my hotel room waiting for the car that was supposed to pick me up and take me to the airport when I received a call that the flight had been delayed a few hours. One of the writing sessions over that time had us asking questions about our relationship with Christ. It was a beautiful focus on our families of origin and when it was that we knew we had come into this relationship with our Savior.

I come from a large family. I would like to keep the anonymity of my siblings, but suffice to say, with seven adults each one of us made choices that directed our free will differently. There were some wonderful choices and some very hard and dark ones that we had witnessed in each other's lives over the years. I found it amazing that we shared the same mother and father, came from the same womb, and yet ended up so different. It made me realize that this powerful gift of free will was both a blessing and at times a burden.

Within those couple of hours, I had taken this incredible life of my own as well as the lives of my siblings and was able to craft it into a song that hopefully would help others discover how they could use their gifts from God. It was crazy that by the time the car picked me up, the song was finished. That was one of the reasons that I enjoyed belonging to the Gospel Music Association. To be able to do writing workshops together with other composers and artists, especially Christians, really felt like it brought out the best in all of us.

Free Will

You know where we both came from. We lived and grew the same. We had a happy childhood and shared our family's name. Our parents love us each as much and gave us all our need. Why does one grow up with love, another filled with greed? Oh, it's free will. Oh, our free will.

Refrain 1: God gave each of us a free will. The place inside our hearts that can open to His call. We have the right to choose Him, or the things of our own design. Help me, gentle Jesus, loving Jesus, gentle Jesus, to choose you and leave my will behind.

I choose to follow Jesus. You chose a different path. How I wish that you could know just how much He loves you still. No matter what we might have done, He does forgive it all. The question you must ask yourself is how to free your will, how to free your will, how to free your will.

Refrain 2: God gave each of us a free will. The place inside our hearts that can open to His call. We have the right to choose Him, or the things of our own design. Help me, gentle Jesus, forgiving Jesus, loving Jesus, to choose you and leave my will behind.

Take away my free will, oh Lord. Take away my free will. Help me, gentle Jesus, to make my will your own. Help me, gentle Jesus, oh, loving Jesus, take away my free will and make my will your own. Oh, your own.

It was so beautiful and empowering to know that this music could be used as a tool of our Lord to reach hearts in such an important focus. I flew back to Scottsdale so excited to begin scheduling life-focused events. It felt like Christmas morning when that first shipment of the CDs and cassettes arrived! My pastor was so complimentary at Mass that weekend when he asked me to share an announcement about the completion of the new project. These affirmations were gifts from God to let me know I was on track and in accord with his will. I had to keep reminding myself that first I belong to God, then I am a wife and mother, and then the ministry. Priorities needed to stay in focus.

Chapter 8

There was always this nagging feeling that a part of me was missing when I was out doing the concert engagements. One really powerful event was in Seattle, Washington. I was at a church named after Saint Philomena. It was near the town where two of our dear friends resided. We met in Germany while in the military community. Mike and Cindy were at the event, and it made me miss Kurt all the more. It just felt like he should be there. But there was an overwhelming feeling in the air that evening. There was so much hunger to feel Christ present. There was such a need for healing for one young girl who was going through a brutal cancer treatment. There was a couple near the front of the audience who was looking so broken. (They reminded me of Kurt and me when we'd come home from Germany.) The church was filled with people, and by the end of the evening I was both exhilarated and exhausted. The focus of cherishing life that evening went so far beyond words. It was coming out of my heart and soul. I was longing for everyone in that church to feel the proof of God's love in and through them. As I sang "Kateri" that evening, I felt the tears of both sorrow and joy run down my face. The sorrow was that I could see certain expressions in the faces of those present, but I couldn't physically be there for each of them as they carried their burdens. There was sorrow for my sister who had done the best and only thing she could do for her infant daughter as she placed her for adoption out of love. So many times, the right things can cause the greatest sorrows. The tears of joy were for those present who throughout the evening began to literally reach out to each other. The couple in the front row embraced and let their own tears flow.

I loved being able to speak about the beauty of life and, between the songs, give examples of how my daughters used to go with me to places like Planned Parenthood as we would witness for life. They would simply sit and play with their dolls while we adults would make ourselves available to women so they would know that someone cared about them and their unborn child. The simple lesson of just being present could make such a difference. I shared about my two saints in heaven, Timmy and Clancy, though I had not yet written their song. I simply told the people there that night how much these tiny precious baby saints were loved.

The next year and a half flew by. Life in our household was sometimes chaotic with children in elementary, middle, and high schools all at the same time. I continued to work on staff at St. Joan of Arc while doing a couple of out-of-town events each month. Kurt accepted a promotion at work to the ACJIS (Arizona Criminal Justice Information System) network for the highway patrol and was really focused on his advancing career.

There were times when I wished it could be like it was in Flagstaff at Nativity BVM when Kurt was playing guitar with me and we would sing together. Now, whenever I would ask if we could do that, the answer was usually that a different priority was more important. I wanted to be most important. I wanted the ministry together to somehow happen. I needed to get back to my daily focus of prayer and spend some quiet time with Jesus in Eucharistic adoration.

In this little room adjacent to the main church is an altar, and on the altar the most beautiful presence of Jesus in a monstrance. A monstrance is made to literally hold Jesus in Holy Communion inside a special glass window so you can see him physically there. One day, I went into the adoration chapel to have a pity party with Jesus. You know what I mean? I knelt down in front of him in exposition of the Blessed Sacrament, cried, and told him all my cares and concerns, waiting to hear the peaceful message that he wanted me to hear.

It was on just such a day when I was bemoaning the totem pole of life having me beneath the children's schedules for school, choir, and baseball; beneath Kurt's work and other priorities; and even, it felt, beneath Tiny, the family beagle.

As I looked into the loving presence of our Lord, I clearly heard a voice speaking into me that said, "I love you, my child." I wept. Then I did a double take when the voice continued, "It is going to get worse before it gets better."

What?! It is going to what? I almost ran out, but then I heard the most beautiful melody and lyric filling the place. It was like angels were singing with me as I heard the song "Mercy" flow out of me, out of him through me.

Mercy

Fall into the ocean of my mercy, the waves will lift and catch you as
you fall. Dive into the river of redemption,
let the running waters carry sin away.

Refrain: Drink deeply at this fountain of salvation. Life-giving
waters springing forth to life anew. Holding, lifting, cleansing, filling,
bringing life anew, the ocean of my mercy.

As the blood and water poured out from the side of my Lord, as
He died for you and me. He brought forth the only source of hope
and healing for this world so much in need. (Refrain)

I see you, oh Lord, my precious Savior. I see You, oh Savior of my
soul. I see you ever-present in this temple, oh My Lord,
complete and whole. (Refrain)

I was quite overwhelmed at the lyric of the song. You see, I was beginning to have feelings for someone during the months preceding this visit with the Lord. Each time I would ask my husband if we could do something together with the music and ministry, he would say no—not out of any ill-intent, but simply he was busy with work and wanting to go back to school for a business degree. But each time I asked my friend if he was available for one of the ministry events or to listen through music with me, he was always there.

When I look back, I can see how the evil one could take a decent and good friendship and the Sacrament of marriage and begin to twist and mutilate it into a broken and sinful focus. I felt like the compass of my life was no longer pointed north. When I realized that my feelings for my friend were developing into more than friendship, I remember asking Kurt if he thought it was possible for someone to love two people at the same time. He said he really didn't know how to answer me and honestly brushed it off.

Just the fact that we had that short but obviously disturbing conversation, I felt the absolute need to go to my pastor and seek the Sacrament of Reconciliation. He is a good man and a good priest. He heard my confession with the tenderness and love of Jesus. I heard him as he spoke the words of absolution, "I absolve you of your sin, in the name of The Father and of The Son and of The Holy Spirit."

I literally wept with relief that I had been able to tell the Lord how sorry I was for where I had let my heart and emotions go for those months. Then when I had said Amen and he said, "Go in the peace of Christ," he asked if I had a minute to chat.

I sat back down and the man, priest, and friend all in one person, told me that I had better get my head out of my backside and start living like I knew I was supposed to be living. I believe the term is tough love, and I needed it. I thank God to this day for that conversation and accountability with someone who cared enough about my soul to make sure I did not mess things up any further.

Now to clarify, I had never crossed the line of any inappropriate physical interaction with my friend, but my heart and soul were guilty of the sin of adultery. I am in constant gratitude that God brought me through that time unscathed and healed. I knew as much as I was now in a better state of grace with Christ, I needed to make things right with my husband, too.

Kurt and I sought counseling and tried to learn better ways of communicating. We went a few times to pick up some tools to put into our marriage toolbox, but we didn't really use them. One of the things learned in hindsight after that counseling was the need to find the right emotional and spiritual direction in our life. We needed a Christian counselor.

The counselor we met with was giving us very worldly focused goals and strange communication techniques. When I asked her how many years she had been married, she said, "In this marriage three years, but all together I have been married twelve years. So believe me I know how to be married." I asked her to explain and she said she had been married three time before. So now on her fourth marriage, she felt like she had the "experience" to tell us how to have a good marriage. She knew how to be divorced, not married. We needed some real skills and a shared prayer life in addition to our individual prayer life. That would come later. Things would indeed get worse before they got better.

In the year 2000, I was invited to do a concert tour in the Holy Lands with the Hosanna 2000 worldwide pilgrimage. The song "Mercy" that the Lord had given me during my pity party with him had really touched the heart of the pilgrimage director, and she told me that I just had to come and represent the United States. I was so excited I couldn't even put it into words.

Of course, I asked Kurt to go with me since I could bring one person. He said he just could not take the time off from work. I was disappointed of course, but I knew that the other person I would ask to go was our daughter Heidi. It is always hard when you want to be able to take everyone, but you can only bring one. Our Edel had been doing really well in her school choir and was going to go on a cruise, so it only felt right to give Heidi the opportunity.

Just two weeks before I left on the concert tour, I had a visit from the religious education director, Sam, in my office at St. Joan of Arc. He told me they had come up with the theme and visual they wanted to use for the children who would be making their first Reconciliation in the following month. He described it as this: "Imagine you come up to a large crevice and on this side it says 'sin' and way across on the other side is the word 'salvation.' The only way to cross the huge chasm is to go over the physical cross of Jesus." The imagery is literally the cross standing in the gap, and the crossbeam is the bridge to walk across to the other side. I totally got what he was suggesting, and within about 20 minutes I had the lyric written.

This was around 9:30 in the morning. By 3:30 that afternoon, I had to go home and clear my head. I had been working on melodies all day and nothing felt right. I was actually getting really frustrated this melody was just not happening for me. As I walked through the front door, I heard Edel playing the piano. It was a beautiful and full melody that I had not heard before.

As she finished playing, I asked her what song it was. She said, "I've been playing it all day since 9:30 this morning. It is a melody I just came up with." The lyric I had written and her melody fit like a glove. She agreed to the co-write of the song, and we named it "The Bridge." What a lovely way the Holy Spirit had used the two of our talents that day. I knew this one would be perfect for the parish as well as the upcoming concert tour in the Holy Lands. God is so good! I felt like I was taking a part of Edel with me.

The Bridge

Come and cross the distance,
Come to me and be the children I have called you to be.
Freed from sin and suffering, freed to love again.
Come and cross this bridge to me and start to live, my friend.

Refrain: The bridge I built goes from the earth and reaches to the
sky above. It reaches far beyond the sins that bind. It reaches
right, it reaches left, just as my arms for you.
Come and cross this bridge to me. My blood was shed for you.

Cleansing waters rushing flow beneath this bridge.
Simply let your sins fall into it.
Water freely flowing here carries them away.
Let all your sins and doubts come to me this way.

SPOKEN: *As the cross was built the center pole reaching from the earth to the sky was the very tree on which our Savior was to be hung. The crossbeam that he carried held also the weight of our sin, the weight of our guilt, the weight of our offenses. And His arms, stretched far to the right and far to the left, were nailed to this beam and He was lifted up to complete the cross. As the last of his blood was shed, water poured forth from the wound in his side and he washed away our sin and brought salvation to a world in need. (Refrain)*

Two weeks later, Heidi and I arrived in Tel Aviv, Israel. As we landed and looked out the window of the airplane, Heidi sounded so upset as she simply said three words, "Stupid palm trees." I cracked up and asked her when she had developed such a dislike of palm trees. She said she just could not stand palm trees ever since we moved to Scottsdale.

What started with such a silly statement upon landing would very quickly be let go of as she and I spent the next two weeks going deep into this amazing place where we would experience Scripture come to life. I could probably write an entire book about this trip, but I just want to share with you a few of the more special moments.

In Bethlehem, the concert was themed "Mother and Child," and it was just wonderful that Heidi, with her lovely voice, was going to sing a duet with me at this event. Yes, both of my daughters have the lovely gift of music, singing, and playing instruments. During the early part of each day, we artists would have to be part of sound checks and stage setups and then, time permitting, we would have some pretty amazing private visits at the various holy sites.

In Bethlehem, however, it was a bit more difficult to be able to go down into the lower level of the Church of the Nativity of Jesus outside of regular visitation times. I was getting really frustrated at how long the concert setup and sound checks were taking because I really wanted to spend some time in this special place. This church was built over the very site where Mother Mary gave birth to Jesus. It is this incredible place where the savior touched earth outside of Mary's womb for the first time. In the life of Christ, there is so much focus on his teaching and his crucifixion, death, and resurrection, but we only think of his birth at Christmas. This joyous place was one at which I wanted to spend some time.

Finally, we were done with the sound setup. Heidi and I walked up to the gate leading to the lower level as it was being locked. The priest noticed my face, saw how sad I was, and asked what was wrong. I said, "I wanted so badly to spend some time here, but our sound checks went too long."

He smiled and then said, "Don't be sad, I have the keys." Then he unlocked the gate and allowed Heidi and me to have a private hour sitting in the little grotto.

To be able to sit there in the quiet was such an amazing gift. Normally, the crowds of people trying to push in and have a look, touch that tender sacred spot, and take a picture make it chaotic. Here we were, just the two of us, sitting and experiencing the very place where heaven touched earth as God incarnate, born of Mother Mary was wrapped in swaddling clothes and laid in the manger. It was such a lovely, quiet, and tender time with my daughter. To this day, it still feels surreal that we had the private time of prayer and contemplation in such a holy place.

The concerts that I had the privilege of being a part of were in over a dozen of the holy sites that pilgrims visit when they go. To sing in the thousands-of-years-old amphitheaters, in the churches that stand over the places of such importance in the life of Christ, Mama Mary, and those early apostles and disciples, and even on the stages that were set up so that thousands of people could come and share the joy of the Jubilee year was beyond thrilling.

The stage that was set up at the site of the Jordan River, where John baptized Jesus, is where I sang "Mercy." That song resonates with me in so many ways. I realized the sin and sadness I was in when I wrote it and heard the words of Jesus's love for me, encouraging me to fall into the ocean of his merciful love and turn from sin. This grace-filled ballad that he used to have me invited to this trip and concert tour of a lifetime was a pure gift.

As I was dunked under the waters of the Jordan River three times as a reminder of my infant baptism, I could feel the cleansing and life-giving grace of our Lord flowing over, around, and through me. God would use this song as a tool of grace for me in the near future.

On Pentecost Sunday as part of the concert tour, we were at the church in the Garden of Gethsemane for Mass and a concert. This garden is where Jesus Christ was just before he was taken away to be crucified. It was where he showed his humanity so powerfully when he prayed to God, the Father, and allowed the extreme anxiety he was feeling to be shared. He prayed that the cup he was about to drink, the agony of the crucifixion and death, could pass by if it be God's will. To know that Christ, being both human and divine, gave in completely to the will of the Father is intense. To know exactly what he was going to go through, the pain, agony, and utter abandonment by his followers, was crushing. His love for all of us is so pure, so unselfish. From this garden, he did indeed go forward to give his life for us. This garden is an incredible place.

I had written the song "Breath of God" for Pentecost the year prior and of course was asked to sing it here. As I began to play the piano intro, I had that familiar feeling of the Holy Spirit taking over my speech. It was different this time in that the words coming out of me sounded like languages here on earth. I did not know what I was saying until I heard the phrase in German *atem des Gottes* coming out of me and understood it to mean "Breath of God."

The priest who was the spiritual director for the tour and pilgrimage asked me how many languages I spoke. Apparently, I had spoken that beautiful phrase in Hebrew, Aramaic, an Old French tongue, German, Latin, Spanish, and English. It was just phenomenal to realize all those languages coming out of my mouth on Pentecost Sunday in the Garden of Gethsemane were all asking for the Breath of God to fill and renew those who could hear. I knew when the time came to record that song, I would absolutely sing it that way.

Breath of God

(Spoken) Ruach Eloim, Nashema Eloim, Souffle de Dieu, Alito del dio, Atem des Gottes, Respiracao do dues, Respiracion del Senor, Adonai, Breath of God, Veni Sancte Spiritu, Ven Espiritu Sancto, Come Holy Spirit.

1. Breath of God, blowing through creation,
filling every nation with the strength of your spirit
Fill me. Use me. Touch me. Love me.

2. Twelve of them in the upper room, praying you'd be coming soon
with the strength of your spirit.
Jesus come, Jesus come, Spirit with Him one.

3. Tongues of fire, burning deep inside our hearts, telling us the
place to start to spread the word of Jesus. No fear here,
no fear here. You are near. You are here.

Bridge: Spirit, Paraclete, Breath of our God, strong driving wind, tongues of fire, God's own desire.
Heaven's dove, Jesus love.

4. We are here, not the twelve, but many, praying you'll be coming soon. Strengthen us to live for You. Fill us. Use us. Touch us. Love us.

5. Breath of God, blowing through creation, filling every nation with the strength of your spirit. Fill me. Use me. Touch me. Love me.

The final concert was the Peace Concert in Jerusalem. How very strange that an event with that name had both Palestinian and Israeli soldiers in uniform and armed to the hilt on both sides of the stage overlooking the city. Peace was the theme and yet as I sang, my heart was heavy knowing that sad and angry discord of so many who live in the Holy Lands.

When it was time to return home, I knew that Heidi and I both came home with a deeper appreciation of Holy Scripture and our deep Judeo roots. I am not exaggerating one bit when I say that every single time I am at Mass somewhere on this planet and I hear the name of one of the places Heidi and I visited together, I see her face and I smile. I remember the way her face looked at each of the holy sites and I am right back there with her watching her go deeper into her faith. Christ gave us such a deep and lasting gift of His precious Word in that powerful trip to Israel together. I had expected to learn much about the life of Jesus. What his life as a Jewish man would have been like and more about the actual journey to and through Jerusalem, Calvary, the crucifixion, death, and resurrection. I learned more than I had expected, and it truly was transformative.

What I did not expect was to fall deeper in love with my sweet Mama Mary. I have always honored her and desired her intercession, but it was incredible to learn about her life and to go deeper with her. The more I learned about her and her life, the more I fell in love with her Son. She is truly pure grace and goodness while at the same time a witness of extreme piety and powerful strength given in unconditional love.

Chapter 9

As I spent those two weeks in the Holy Lands, the music writing became more intense, especially as I had time in Eucharistic adoration in the little churches and big ones alike. Just being there affected me like never before. I came home ready to go back into the recording studio at Gaithers for the next project, *The Bridge*.

The songs that became part of *The Bridge* all had to do with the incredible mercy that Jesus offers us. The ways that we take in his Word and listen and hopefully respond were all incorporated into this project.

One of the songs I remember writing while I was sitting there in the Holy Lands was a song called "Speak To Me." It was awe-inspiring to be in these different holy places where Jesus had lived, began his ministry, and ultimately given his life for us. And somehow the Old Testament came closer into focus, which surprised me.

For some reason, Elijah became part of my journey. I think of Elijah and the way that he was so willing to serve God, even in the midst of the incredible trials that he was under. There was that point when he was in the desert, and he was wishing that he could just sit down under the furze tree and die. He said to God, "Could I just have you end my life, Lord?"

And it had reminded me of a homily that I had heard from a dear priest friend, Father JT, where he said we literally are given the opportunity to hear God speak to us but because of so much busyness and loudness in the world, God's voice is so often pushed out.

But that day, instead of being released from his life, God sent him angels. He literally sent Elijah angels to bring him food and water and to attend to his needs. And then nourished and strengthened, Elijah continued the journey until he found himself at Mount Horeb. And it was there that he encountered God very differently.

We think of the stories in Scripture where Moses encountered God in the burning bush. Noah, of course, built the ark and then the flood came after he was obedient. He looked ridiculous to his community until the rain came. So many of the prophets looked ridiculous. So many of those who are called to serve God with their life look ridiculous. There are times when I felt ridiculous.

There was such a wonderful reminder as I sat there and wrote the song "Speak To Me," asking God to literally continue speaking to me. Up until this point, my childhood encounters with God's Word, in that language that again seemed so foreign but was so intimate and familiar in my soul, were not clear in their meaning. Now, the encounters with God speaking to me were becoming so much more real, so much more in my language. I remember as I penned the song "Speak To Me," I was literally asking God to keep doing this. To speak into my life.

When I finished writing it, I was kind of excited! My daughters were now in their teen years and honestly some pretty good critics. I remember playing the song for Edel and asking for her opinion. It was funny when she said that she heard Father JT's homily as well. She asked me why I wrote such a big song when God was coming to us in the quiet whispers like Elijah experienced on Mount Horeb.

I, of course, went back to the piano and sat down. I thought about Elijah again standing there at Mount Horeb and experiencing the loud driving wind, the earthquake, the fire, and the rumble of the mountain. But then in the tiny, whispering breeze he realized that God was present. He came to the entrance of the cave and stood there and said, "Speak, Lord, I'm willing to continue serving you." So I went to the piano and sat down and the song "Whispers" came out.

Whispers

Come to me in the silence. Whisper my name.
In the quiet of the twilight. In the gentle fall of rain. Oooh, oooh.

In the lulling roll of thunder, on a gentle breeze.
Talk to my heart, Lord. Set my soul at ease. Oooh, oooh.

Like Elijah on Mt. Horeb, I thought you had to
come like a roaring lion,
But you simply came as love.

Not in the roaring ocean, not in a raging storm,
But in a single sunbeam on an early summer morn.

Speak to me softly. Whisper my name.
Since you've touched my heart, Lord, I'll never be the same.
Oooh, oooh.

Now as a mother of teenagers, I felt such tenderness in my heart that my daughter would ask me to play that song for her every night for the next couple of months before she would go to sleep at night. She would go to sleep with the words of the song asking God to whisper to her, and from the moment he would touch her heart with his word, all would be changed forever.

And now that the songs were complete, it was time to go back to the Gaither Studios in Indiana. The band that I had worked with so well on the *Kateri* record was ready, and it was time to get this next recording done. Once again, I was tremendously blessed with these professional session players, who brought their A game to my lyric and melodies.

This project went so much deeper than the one before. Something about mercy resonated so much with me because of the experiences from which the songs arose. To acknowledge my sinfulness, to seek and receive God's forgiveness, and then to offer it all back to him made such a difference. Because these were being written from my real-life experiences and from those intimate moments with Jesus in the adoration chapel, there was something uniquely beautiful about this project.

When I speak about the intimate moments in the adoration chapel with Jesus, I really do literally mean time with Jesus. The funny thing was, up to this point, when I would go to Eucharistic adoration at St. Joan of Arc Church, the associate pastor, Father JT, unbeknownst to me had noticed the little bag that I took with me to the chapel. In my adoration-time bag, I had my Bible, a rosary, a little book entitled *An Hour With Jesus*, and usually at least one book about a saint.

One evening, we invited Father JT to our home for dinner. When he arrived and rang the front doorbell, we opened the door and invited him in. Before he came into the house though, he asked if he could borrow a rosary. I thought it was kind of strange, but I went into the house and brought the rosary out to him since he had not yet come into the house. He literally stood outside the front door and prayed silently a decade, which is 10 Hail Mary prayers. I stood there quietly, just kind of watching him.

Then he handed the rosary back to me and said, "There, that's better." He came just inside the front door, and I offered him a beverage. He didn't answer but instead asked if he could borrow a Bible. I'm not quite sure what he thought he was going to be experiencing in our home such that he needed such a covering of prayer, but I went in to the living room, got the Bible, and handed it to him. He opened it and stood there, again silently, reading Scripture for a good five minutes. He then closed the Bible, handed it back to me, and asked me, "Was that awkward?"

I said, "Yes, it was very awkward!"

He simply said, "Now you know how you make Jesus feel."

It was like a lightbulb clicked on in my head and my heart at the same moment. I realized how busy I was when I had such a marvelous opportunity to just sit with God and listen. The way that I approached Eucharistic adoration after that evening was to simply go into the chapel and literally lie face down on the floor in front of Jesus. I would stay in that position, lying prostrate, for 15 or 20 minutes.

Then I would move to a chair, and the only thing that I brought with me was a notebook and a pen. I would look into the face of my Lord and I would ask him what he wanted to share with me. So many of the songs written from that day forward have happened in the adoration chapel.

I think we forget that God continues to speak to us today just as he did to Elijah and Abraham and Isaiah and other people before us. They learned how to quiet themselves and listen. If you take nothing else from the rest of this book, I hope you take time alone with Jesus. He loves you so much and he has so much that he wants to share with you if you will just come to him and listen. Your heart and mind and soul will be overwhelmed with the beauty that He will pour into you.

Much of what I've written over the years no one else has heard. Just me and Jesus. The songs that I have felt called to share over the years are the ones that have been recorded and shared around the country.

***

I was pleasantly surprised and so grateful when I went back to some of the churches that I had been to previously with the first record *Kateri*. It was beautiful to see the reactions of people.

One that stands out happened just outside of Seattle. As I mentioned, I had been there previously with the concert about life, and now I was there with the new project, *The Bridge*. As the concert that evening came to a close, a young woman walked up to me. She asked me if I remembered being there for the life concert previously and I said yes. She went on to tell me that it had been a Friday evening. She said the song "Kateri" had affected her deeply. She took a couple of moments to kind of compose herself, as her emotions seemed pretty raw. And then she said that on Saturday morning, she was scheduled to have an abortion. But after coming to that event and hearing "Kateri," instead she went home and told her mother that she was pregnant. And then she asked me if I would like to meet her son.

A woman older than her was standing just a few feet away holding an infant in her arms. I got to hold that infant. When I got back to my hotel room that night, I knelt down and wept tears of joy. I thanked God for the precious beauty that I had been privileged to experience that night. I came home from that trip and told Kurt that if I never sing another song or write another melody that the ministry would be complete.

Also, upon my return home, I sent a copy of the *Kateri* CD to the adoption agency in Utah along with a letter to Lori's daughter. I prayed she would receive it someday and know the impact her life had made on another, and how much she is loved by her birth mom and also by me by just being herself. She affected my heart so deeply, and I had never met her.

As an artist and a speaker, you don't always get such concrete affirmation of the work that is being done by the Holy Spirit. I have never really felt worthy of doing this in my life. I think many times people who claim the title "Christian recording artist" don't really understand what it is they're supposed to be doing. When I look back on how I was raised and the fact that I did not study music formally, I must acknowledge it is all gift. Yes, I was raised by a musician. Yes, I went to Blue Lake Fine Arts Camp as a young lady with my flute, but the songs that God has given me are nothing short of a gift. And then the way that he has allowed professional session musicians and the studios to make such a difference, to make the music even more beautiful, is all part of his plan.

For the next couple of years, I saw how these two projects, *Kateri* and *The Bridge* were wonderful tools of the Holy Spirit. As people heard the various songs and why they were written, my ministry boundaries expanded. The way people began to share their stories with me helped to affirm why I had been called to this itinerant life.

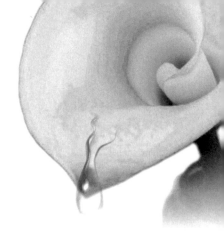

Chapter 10

When I think of some examples in the way that the Holy Spirit continued to use these heartfelt projects, I have to share about what happened on 9/11/2001. I know everyone has a memory of where they were and what they were feeling when that horrific attack against humanity happened. I have such mixed feelings about that day. It took years before I was able to share what had happened with me personally.

I had been asked to do a filming with CatholicTV in Boston and was very excited to do so. Their staff and I figured out the best dates and they booked my flights on American Airlines. I was to fly in, do my filming with them, and then fly home on Tuesday, September 11 on Flight 11 from Logan International Airport. To get home earlier in the day, it was to be a direct flight to Los Angeles and then a short hop to Phoenix. I had my regular aisle seat ticketed and was ready to go.

A little over a week prior to the scheduled filming, they called and asked if I could come early since they had a crew that was coming in for a number of other shows to be filmed and even with the ticket changes, it would be more cost effective. My husband and I talked about it and even though it was on our wedding anniversary, it felt like we should go ahead and agree to the change of dates.

They changed my tickets. I went a week earlier to film and flew home on Tuesday, September 4 instead of the 11th. Kurt was at his office at the Department of Public Safety when the first plane hit the tower in New York City. He called me and told me to keep our children home that day. Something was up. I turned on the television and watched in horror as the rest of the news unfolded.

When they began talking about American Airline Flight 11 out of Boston, I felt such a wave of emotion. I was relieved to be sitting in my living room hugging my children and at the exact same moment I had such guilt. I prayed to God that my seat had not been sold to anyone else after my dates had changed for the trip. To know that my life had literally been spared by God as CatholicTV asked me to reschedule and my husband's openness to celebrating our anniversary a few days late all became such great favor in my life.

When I hear the phrase survivor guilt, it takes me back to this day; instead of allowing the darkness to win, I pray. I pray for the repose of the souls who perished that day. I pray for the families and friends who lost loved ones. I pray that I will do what God wants me to do since he saw fit to keep me here. Not just because I am a wife, many wives died that day. Not just because I am a mother, again too many moms died that day. But for whatever purpose God decided to keep me here.

I see this as one more way to connect with the communion of saints. Each and every one of us is called to fulfill the life God created us for and then to go home to him to share in everlasting life with our creator.

Just a few days after that horrific attack, I was scheduled for a lovely event in Mandeville, Louisiana. It was such a God thing that what was supposed to be an artist development trip ended up being an evening of prayer and healing.

Kitty Cleveland is a Catholic singer-songwriter whom I met in Washington D.C., where I was singing at the UCMVA (United Catholic Music & Video Association) Unity Awards. She told me about a CD that she recorded. After listening to it, I was absolutely blown away by the beauty of her voice and the sincerity of her heart for ministry. She wanted to host a concert in her parish in Mandeville so that we could bring an evening of reflection through music and spoken word there.

She also offered to open for me, so I would be able to watch the way that she presented. Then she would watch the way that I presented. After the concert and really looking closely at how the evening was received, we planned to take a couple of days and do a workshop. Our hope was that we could see what worked best given her presentation style and to find concrete ways of moving her ministry forward.

Of course, with the attack that Tuesday, all of the airports in the country were shut down. As they began to open on Friday, it was quite a feat to say the least.

I had a call from America West Airlines. They asked me what my purpose of travel was to Louisiana. I explained that I was going there to do an event of ministry in the Catholic Church, an evening of music and prayer. I was scheduled to fly on Friday afternoon. They called me back and said that they would indeed get me to Louisiana on time since they felt that was an extremely important event. I would, however, be flying on Saturday morning.

When I arrived at the airport, it was a strange atmosphere to say the least. People were cautious and anxious to be on their way for sure. What was honestly crazy though, were those who took issue with the inspections, having seemed to disregard what happened only a few days prior. They were upset and agitated because everyone had to have their belongings searched before going anywhere near the gates and planes.

When I boarded my plane, there was a gentleman sitting across the aisle from me who was wearing a turban on his head. I have to admit I felt a little bit nervous. I was upset with myself for having that feeling of judgment of another human being. And yet I am a human being, and I couldn't help feeling what I was feeling.

Then my codependent side, wanting to make sure that everyone was happy, kicked in. Since I was sitting in the first-class section of the aircraft, everyone who came onto the airplane walked past me. They would look at me, they would look across the aisle at the man with the turban, and I felt the need to say good morning to him. "This is a good day, isn't it?" I was coming up with a hundred little comments to try to put people at ease. I wish I had a video of what I looked and sounded like. It would be hilarious to watch now.

I called Kurt from my cell phone and I spoke quietly so that no one else could hear me. I explained the situation and that I had a few butterflies in my stomach. My husband, who many times uses comedy to help me relax, said, "If when you are getting ready to take off, you hear the captain say [now imagine hearing his best Middle Eastern man's voice] 'ladies and gentlemen, welcome aboard this flight to Louisiana,' then maybe you want to get off the plane." So I had a little chuckle and then relaxed as we finished the boarding process.

We went through the normal routine of seatbelt checks and tray tables and all the instructions that flight attendants normally do. And then we were ready to take off. As we were approaching full takeoff speed near the end of the runway, the pilot told us to assume the crash position. Now in all the years that I have been flying, I've never heard that before or since. It was crazy how everyone on that plane just instinctively knew to lean forward with our heads down near our knees and wait.

The aircraft made the most horrendous screeching noise as the pilot aborted the takeoff and was trying to stop the plane before we were out onto the highway around the airport. It was an absolutely terrifying feeling. The rumbling and the screeching of the tires as it came down hard on the runway shook the entire aircraft as we stopped. My heart was pounding so fast I swear I could hear it.

It was only a few minutes, but it felt like a long time before the pilot came on and said, "I am sorry about that, folks. We had no other option but to abort the takeoff. There was a malfunction in one of the crucial instruments and had we taken off, it would've been really, really bad." They limped the airplane back to the gate. After a few minutes, they began the process of unloading the passengers back into the terminal and then brought a different aircraft over. With everyone across the country displaced and trying to get people to the destinations that had been canceled the previous days because of the attack on our country, it was nothing short of chaotic.

We finally had another aircraft and it was time to re-board; again, the man sitting across the aisle wearing his turban was getting horrible looks from the passengers coming on board. What a strange day it turned out to be. What was amazing is that even though I was leaving a day later than planned and now was extremely delayed, I got to New Orleans in time to be met by my driver and taken to Mandeville just in time for the concert of healing to begin.

It was beautiful to hear Kitty's voice begin that concert. Hearing the beautiful grace flow out of this lady was exactly what I needed to calm my nerves before I would be any good for her community. As was the case with churches all over the country, this church was filled to standing room only. In the face of such calamity, pain, and suffering, people turn to God.

I have prayed since that day that we would never have to feel such darkness and agony in order to have full churches. It seems like we all need to be on our knees acknowledging our need for God. My prayer in ministry has always been to allow the grace of God to flow in everyday life. To find him in the joys, not just the sorrows. To find him in each and every moment of every day. Just like the little nuns in Gallup, New Mexico had taught me years before.

The next couple of days, Kitty and I worked well together. It was wonderful to be able to share this gift of ministry with someone who wanted to learn and give in return. Believe it or not, this life can be very lonely. It is strange to think that even though you are in front of hundreds and at times thousands of people, you can feel alone. In front of is not the same as being next to someone and sharing a life and a ministry. Then sadly, many people who claim to be Christian artists are so self-centered they don't want to share anything with anyone, even if it may be to their good. I have never understood that mindset. I felt that when God opens a door for me, I should hold it open for the next person coming through.

Since then, I have worked with a number of artists who were beginning a ministry that included music and spoken word. I look back on the time with Kitty and I am grateful for the true beauty that exuded from this woman. It has always been my joy to share the gifts that God has given me with others. When I saw the open and joyful way that Kitty received what I had to offer, it made that trip worth the extra effort.

I knew, too, upon my arrival home from this trip that God was indeed calling me to the next level of ministry. I wasn't just supposed to learn for myself to share a life of ministry, but I was called to assist others along the way. It was time to consider leaving my work at St. Joan of Arc Parish. It was with mixed feelings that I was leaving parish work, even though by now it was almost half itinerant ministry and half parish music leadership.

Once again, though, God made it easy for me. When the decision was made that I was no longer going to be on staff at St. Joan of Arc, we made the announcement to the parish that I would be finishing my last couple of weeks with them. I felt loved to the moon and back by the community. The musicians that I had had such a lovely time leading and directing over those years really made me feel like I would be missed.

What made it simple for me to be able to leave were a few of the comments that people made to me. I am sure that they meant well but it was so strange to hear phrases like, "We are going to miss you because you are the main reason that we have been coming to Mass here." I thought that if there was such focus on the music during Mass instead of on the physical presence of Jesus Christ in his Word and in the Eucharist, then something was out of order.

The affirmation was a good thing. I was able to lovingly have conversations with people about how although music is important in liturgy, the most important and only important thing is that they hear and respond to the Word of God and make sure that they have opened their hearts to the knowledge of the Eucharist.

The only sad part of no longer leading music there was that the new director who came on board for the contemporary music department felt uncomfortable when I was there to attend Mass with my family. He literally asked the pastor to speak with me about going to a different parish.

God used this insecurity for a beautiful purpose, though. Our family made the decision to become parishioners at Blessed Sacrament parish in Scottsdale. It became our new parish home, and it has been and continues to be a perfect fit. This incredible community prays for Kurt and me constantly. I don't know of any other community that would have someone gone as often as I am and still make me feel like I am completely part of the family and at home when I am there. The notes, cards, emails, and phone calls to remind me that they are praying for me is one of the beautiful graces that God allows to surround me.

Chapter 11

Life feels like a tapestry. We share this journey in ways we can't possibly plan for or fully understand. Each of us is one of the threads that when woven together make the cloth whole. And just when we think we have seen the beauty of the journey, we have an experience that turns it over and reveals its full expression and clarity. Just like a tapestry.

When I think of the people who are the threads of the tapestry of my life, it is overwhelming. There are no coincidences when it comes to living a life of grace. Every person in every situation that God has allowed reveal His grace in deeper and more meaningful ways.

Rick and Linda Elias are two of these beautiful people. Linda would tell Rick he needed to reach out to me to see what we could be doing together. At the same time, Kurt was telling me to call Rick to see what we should be doing together. I honestly don't remember who called whom first. But I am so glad we connected. It was like traveling with a brother, albeit a crazy, let's-try-anything-in-music kind of brother. Plus, we were able to share our individual journeys in our Catholic faith.

God blessed the work we did together so well. We must be up to 2002 or 2003 by this point. I remember receiving a phone call from a recording artist who lived in the Phoenix Valley. He asked me if I had a date open on my calendar. He had been approached by a group from Midland, Texas, who were looking for a Catholic artist to sing and lead ministry for an event. He was booked but wanted to make sure that I was able to go instead.

My calendar was open for the date, and I contacted the event coordinators. They were so happy that I was able to come. It was an event called Faces of the Children, the Persecuted Church in Africa. In addition to bringing an awareness of what was happening to children around the world, this group was doing concrete good work to stop the abuse and human trafficking of children. Bishop Gassis from Africa would also be part of the event.

The more I learned about the impact and the purpose of the event that I was being hired to go and do, the more I wanted to make sure that as many people as possible would attend. I knew that at this point I had been in quite a few states and that quite a few people knew who I was as a recording artist. But I also knew that if there was someone much more well known, it would make the attendance all the better. I had done quite a few events with Rick Elias around the country, and I knew that he would be a great draw for this event as well.

When I discussed this with the event planners, they thought it was a great idea. Rick's music is played all over the world. He is most known for his song "Man of No Reputation" and singing the songs written by Rich Mullins on the *Jesus* record, which he also produced. If you've heard the song "My Deliverer" or "The Prayer of St. Francis," you have heard Rick's voice.

The events we did around the country were very well received. Our styles of music and the way we shared our faith journeys complemented each other well. I have to say it was nice to be partnered with a friend who had also been through some hardships and was able to see God's hand in the midst of it and find a beautiful way to share the story. Music really is a blessing. Being able to trust each other and at the same time encourage each other to keep doing what we feel called to do was a real gift.

Watching Rick figure out who he was as a solo artist again, after touring with Rich Mullins and the Ragamuffins for so long, was a powerful lesson for me. When we arrived in Midland, we felt like we were being greeted by old friends. We even had nicknames, unbeknownst to us until we were met at the airport with signs that read, "Welcome Julie Andrews and Frank Sinatra."

What a privilege to spend those few days together serving the community and bringing the awareness of the world to places that are hurting so deeply. To realize that children are bought and sold like commodities broke my heart. Having young children of my own, I could not imagine the pain and suffering of these little ones or of their parents. Once again, I faced the quandary of the gift that God had given me. What good was it to simply sing about something?

We were at dinner with Bishop Gassis after the events ended. He asked me if I would be willing to go to Africa. I asked him what good would it possibly serve for me to go there. He told me that when he heard me singing, he felt like God had given a special anointing to my voice. He continued to say that if more people would hear it, their hearts would be transformed for good.

Having some good heart-to-heart discussions with Rick about the music and about ministry was a God thing. There were many blessings that would come out of this trip to Midland. One of the couples that I met was Janice and Rhett. They welcomed me to their home. They told me that whenever I would return to Midland that their guesthouse would be my home away from home. Sometimes when you receive an offer like that, it feels like mere words, but with these two it came from their hearts. I knew that our paths were meant to cross. I knew that God had plans that would be revealed, and to go home with that simple knowing was such a great gift.

This couple shared their story with me about their conversion to the Catholic faith. When I saw the exuberance and the joy with which Janice spoke about the Catholic faith, I hoped that my delight was as contagious as hers. And I remember asking Rhett what brought him to the Catholic faith. I was expecting a very emotional and deeply moving story. Instead he simply said the more that he learned about the truth of the Catholic faith, the more that he knew he would simply live the truth. It wasn't so much a conversion as it was a completion of his learning about Christ and living in the faith that Christ started. He was very matter-of-fact and just made you want to be boldly Catholic. I felt like the tapestry of my life was becoming not only stronger with the additional threads being woven through it, but it was becoming more beautiful at the same time.

***

I continued to share about the ways that God is revealed in my life through his sacred word and in the moments of daily living in the way that is captured in my songs. It was awesome to see lives being touched. To know that he had literally spared the life of an unborn child in Seattle made me wonder how many other people were receiving such a blessing from him through my small gift. With the ministry continuing to develop, I had by this time been in most of the states here in the United States as well as Israel in the Holy Lands.

It was in early 2004 when I was asked to go to Oklahoma with a colleague who was helping to open a Rachel's Vineyard retreat center. We were going to do a benefit concert and an evening of reflection on mercy. This retreat is specifically for women and men who chose elective abortion and are now trying to heal emotionally and spiritually.

It was the day before the benefit concert that I was in my hotel and had a rather unpleasant visit shall we say. During the day, we had had wonderful times of prayer and even a holy hour of Eucharistic adoration with Jesus. But it was around two o'clock in the morning when I felt a physical disturbance in my room. All I can really tell you is that I knew evil was physically present.

I called Kurt and asked him to pray with me. The physical reality of Satan is hard to explain. Kurt prayed with me for a while, but I knew that he had to get some sleep because he was caring for our children while I was on this trip.

We rang off, and then I called Kitty Cleveland; she answered and prayed with me as well. She is one of those amazing women who loves and serves the Lord and is open to His will. When the disturbance was finally over and I was able to go back to bed, I realized it was yet another affirmation of the good work that was being done if the evil one hated it so badly. The next evening was powerfully grace filled as people came to learn about the healing that can happen when they reach out and receive the mercy of Jesus. That was in February.

During that horrible encounter with the evil one in my hotel room, I heard a real voice threaten that if I did not stop doing what I was doing, he was going to attack everything that was of great importance in my life.

When I arrived home after this particular trip, I met with my spiritual director. He reminded me of the importance of keeping Sacramentals close at hand. Sacramentals are simple elements of water, oil, or salt that have been blessed by a priest and are indeed holy. Holy water is used when a person is baptized and is powerful in keeping evil away. Blessed salt is also used as an effective tool against evil.

He reminded me of Saint Benedict, who is the father of Western monasticism and someone who, by my oblation, I was trying to include in my life. He reminded me to carry and wear a Saint Benedict medal. I went deeper into my prayer life. I began to spend more hours in Eucharistic adoration, and daily Mass became more important than ever before. And, once again, the melodies and the lyric in the music that I was writing became so much more meaningful and beautiful. I was almost afraid to write some of them down because it felt like I was going to have to go a lot deeper.

I remember one evening in particular trying to talk with my husband about it. I kept remembering the words from when we lived back in Germany and the person who gave us the interpretation of this beautiful spiritual time: When this couple would do this ministry together, it would be more meaningful.

Kurt was in the middle of finishing a business degree. He had received a nice promotion with the highway patrol administration in Phoenix. Our oldest daughter, Edel, was in college by this point. Our middle daughter was a senior in high school. And our son, Paul, was in elementary school at Pope John XXIII Catholic School in Scottsdale. There was a lot going on in our household, and it almost felt like there was a storm brewing. So many beautiful things surrounded us, but I had an underlying feeling of "something."

I came home from Mass and I had the most lovely surprise when I received a phone call and an invitation for me to go to Germany with Youth Arise International. They were going to prepare for World Youth Day that would be hosted in Germany in 2005. I was excited to be asked to be a part of this team.

What you may not realize is that the teams and the people involved in World Youth Day are not funded by anyone financially. All of those folks who go there have to raise money or have their own money in order to be able to do it. And of course, the price tag for this pre-World Youth Day meeting was around $2,000.

When Kurt came home from work that evening, I was so excited. I said I really, really wanted to do it. And when I told him the cost, he said that if it was meant to be then the funds would be there from the ministry. It was amazing that the next morning, when I went to the mailbox for my ministry, there was a check from a couple in Michigan who had been to an event. It was for $2,000 and there was a note attached that said please use this for whatever you would like to be able to do. I was delighted!

Once again, the Holy Spirit was guiding and allowing things to happen. Kurt was excited for me. We made plans, bought my ticket, and before long, it was time for me to go back to Germany. It was a wonderful reminder of the years spent with my husband and children living there. Such a flood of memories of joyful excursions with our friends and children to so many beautiful places. I was reconnecting to the first five years of our marriage and going deeper into my Catholic faith. I felt like God was allowing not only reminders and healings, but revealing a purpose beyond that of World Youth Day.

To be part of the team for Youth Arise International preparing for World Youth Day 2005 was a definite highlight in my ministry. The team that went over to Germany was the most organized and loving group of people I had worked with in a long time. The way they coordinated the youth housing, plans for feeding everyone, Mass locations, and ground transportation was amazing.

While we were there for the planning-session week, we stayed at a beautiful retreat center. To be back in this magnificent country surrounded by such prayerful people with such a great purpose was fantastic. I know this sounds ridiculous in the face of all of the World Youth Day preparations, but such a happy moment for me was when we would have coffee and cakes in the afternoon. That familiar, wonderful German coffee and those delicious German pastries and cakes were like going back to a happy place.

The sisters and priests who ran the retreat center spoke English, but it was so nice to hear the familiar German language again when we were out and about. It was nice to have an overview of what would be happening there in 2005 and know that the powerful and beautiful experiences prepared for the youth were going to be such a gift of grace for them.

Once again, though, I felt like I was only seeing part of the picture; I knew there was something more. When I included Germany on my event calendar, I was contacted by the U.S. military. In Landstuhl, Germany, there is a huge military hospital. I was asked to go and visit with hundreds and hundreds of wounded servicemen and women. This location is a triage hospital for the wounded in Iraq and Afghanistan.

Near the hospital is a place called Fisher House. Fisher House is where family members can stay while their wounded service members are being treated. As beautiful as the experience of prepping for World Youth Day may have been, the heaviness of this visit was almost too difficult. There was an incredible army nurse who accompanied me and led me from room to room during my visit there. He had so much compassion for these brave men and women who had been wounded so badly.

The expressions and the looks on the faces of some of the wounded when they would ask me if I could bring a priest to them is engraved in my mind. They knew I was a Catholic recording artist and that I was there to pray with them, but the deep need in their eyes spoke volumes. What they witnessed, what they experienced, and what some of them had to do was something those of us who have never been downrange will never fully understand.

One young man in particular shared with me his story. He asked if I had heard the Scripture passage in John 20:27 of Jesus telling Thomas to put his finger into the nail marks in his hands and his hand into the wound in his side. I said of course, that I was very familiar with this passage. Then he lifted the side of his shirt, and there was this massive wound that was now healed over if you can call it such. A deep wound in his side.

He explained how he was wounded. The local children would come and make friends with the soldiers. After a number of weeks of exchanging pleasantries, candy, and juice, the children would absolutely be a part of their thoughts and hearts. And one little boy in particular had become friends with this soldier.

A few weeks later, the same little boy came walking into the compound where the soldier was stationed. This compound was full of munitions. The little boy was wearing a full body vest of explosives. The serviceman who watched him walking toward those inside the compound knew that he had no choice but to shoot this child before he came in, as he was literally a walking bomb. As he raised his gun, extending his arm and focusing on what he knew he had to do, he paused for a number of seconds fighting back his emotions. It was during that time, with his arm raised, that the enemy sniper knowing the weak spot of his body armor shot him in the side.

Watching the child obliterated in front of his eyes in the same instance that he felt gunfire in his body was like an explosion inside and outside. Then he held my hand super tight and said, "I need a priest! I need Reconciliation and Peace! Please bring a priest."

This is one story of hundreds and hundreds that I heard those days spent serving those who serve. I was invited to come because I'm a Catholic recording artist, but nothing prepared me for it. Spending time with the families at the Fisher House was the most humbling experience ever. Having been part of the military community many years before, I knew where their hearts were. Once again while doing the concert there, I felt like what I was doing was so small in comparison. They were thanking me for coming and ministering to them by sharing God's love, mercy, and healing. I was so grateful that it was the Holy Spirit who was doing the singing because I felt so insignificant in the face of all of that they were experiencing.

I had been asked before going to Germany to print a large number of headshot photographs and bring Sharpies for autographs. As

I went from room to room and simply wrote "May God bless and heal you" on each of them, it seemed ridiculous. And I have to say, that ever since then, I have never printed headshots for autographing again. It just seems so strange when I see colleagues and other folks who are part of the Christian music world be so enamored with publicity and promotional materials.

It was a strange time. I kept going back to that day in the adoration chapel where I heard the voice of Jesus tell me that things would get worse before they would get better. This had to be the worst. But as I was flying home from Germany, there were quite a number of servicemen and women who were also flying back to the States. They were physically healed and heading home. As a couple of them shared their stories with me and how grateful they were to have visits, I started to feel a little better about why I had been asked to go there in the first place.

I have to say, too, that it was interesting to see my name on the marquee next to Arnold Schwarzenegger, who was visiting at the same time. He has such a large personality and then there is me. I will always hold on to the fact that it was the prayer, that simple portal of grace, that afforded me the privilege of those days.

Chapter 12

I kept hearing the words that it would get worse before it got better. Trying to find joys between events of sadness in life is a real balancing act. My daughter Heidi graduated high school and began college. That was a most joyful celebration. Watching my children enter adulthood and knowing that they are Christian are such sources of pride.

One of my favorite things for both of our daughters was that we got to hang up a poster of their lives in the school hallway on graduation day. Their baby pictures, their baptism and first communion pictures, confirmation pictures, and their various awards throughout high school were emblazoned on a large poster. It is one of those joys that parents just cherish. In the midst of sadness and trials, God is always giving a reason to smile. What amazing young women my daughters are.

Every parent can appreciate the accomplishment achieved when they see the hard work pay off. 2004 really became a defining year. As I have shared in different ministry events since then, it was the year that the gloves came off. It was like watching a spiritual battle between good and evil, between joy and sorrow, between beauty and ugliness. When I thought of those words spoken by Satan, they made me angry.

I tried to keep my focus on my relationship with Christ, my husband, children, and ministry. I knew I was being called to finish writing a few songs and get ready to do another recording. It's funny how something that seems bad in the moment can turn into something absolutely beautiful. With a very busy family life and work life and everything that goes on in a household, it is easy to step on each other's toes. I remember one evening Kurt and I were having an argument about something. You can see how important it was. I can't even remember what the argument was about.

But after a few minutes of disagreement, I remember asking myself: How can I not see the face of God in my husband? He is a baptized Christian and so am I. We regularly go to Mass, receive the Eucharist, and go to Reconciliation, so why am I not seeing the face of God looking back at me right now? And the truth of the matter was that I was not looking for the face of God, I was looking to try to win an argument. The next morning, I really took some time to think about my actions the evening before. That phrase *seeing the face of God* just kept going over and over in my thoughts.

I went to the adoration chapel to do some writing and listening and the song, "The Face of God" came home with me. When we literally think about Christ being present in our day-to-day life, we need to be able to see him in our spouse, in the gift of marriage born as children, in the people God allows us to meet and minister with in our day-to-day. When I say minister, I don't mean like a churchy kind of minister, but rather human beings interacting with other human beings in need. Whether it's holding someone's hand and letting them cry or taking a food box to someone in need or maybe it's just handing a five-dollar bill out the car window when you feel prompted to do so. We are able to see the face of God and care for him as we care for each other.

When Kurt came home from work, I shared the song with him and it was so nice to see his reaction. I don't know if I had written a song just for him before, but this one was definitely his. I love that it became the title track for my next project.

When I was in Indiana at the Gaither Studios recording this project, God gave me yet another little gift of grace along the way. When I was flying out to do the recording, we flew into a snowstorm that forced us to land in Grand Rapids, Michigan, instead of Indianapolis, Indiana. I was able to change my rental car reservation to Grand Rapids and then told the airline that instead of flying home from Indianapolis that it would be better for me to have them do my return from Grand Rapids as well.

When I finished the recording session, I was able to drive up to the little town of Free Soil, Michigan, where I had been raised. Even though I only had 24 hours with my Aunt Lenida and Pa John, it was like the most wonderful gift in the middle of a very busy time.

One of the memories I will absolutely cherish from this sweet visit was that evening when I was getting ready for bed, Auntie came in and literally tucked me in. It was so sweet and so tender. I called Kurt and said, "Guess where I am? I have literally just been tucked into bed so tightly I can barely move."

The next morning when I was getting ready to leave for the airport, my aunt told me that I would not have to buy any of that terrible airport food because she made lunch for me. It was hilarious when we were airborne and I opened up the sack that she had given me. Inside was so much food that there was no way I could ever eat it all. The gentleman sitting to my left looked like he might be a little hungry, so I offered him one of the four sandwiches that my aunt had made for me. Of course, each sandwich came with a pickle, a piece of fruit, and a dessert. The man across the aisle said that he was hungry, too, so he got lunch. And then the man sitting next to him looked across and asked if this was some kind of a magic lunch bag. Believe me when I tell you that the people in first class were missing out big time.

This visit home was such a perfectly timed gift of grace. God knew what was coming for the rest of this year, and he had filled me to the rim with love of my family and a reminder of where my grace began.

The Face of God

I hear Him in the whispers, as we cuddle close at night.
I feel His arms around me as you hold me tight.
I see Him in the morning as I rise and see your face.
Because of you, I know of God's grace.

Refrain: Through the love of man and wife, God manifests His love.
In the beauty of a child He's proven. As we look around the world,
in the eyes of those we meet, we see the face of God.

Tiny fingers reaching, a newborn baby's smile, trusting eyes that
stay with you throughout their lives. The never-ending courage,
knowing love will see them through, a gift from God to you.

Bridge: Homeless, tired, searching souls in need.
Hungry, lonely, suffering, Christ in those in need.
Ooooh, Aaaah, Ooooh. (Refrain)

The next thing that we would experience as a family in 2004 was what would happen to our daughter Edel. She has given me permission to share her part of our journey as a family. Just days before her 20th birthday, she was invited to hang out by a young lady with whom she'd gone to high school. The plan was that they would go to her grandmother's house, have dinner, and watch movies and stuff. On the way there, however, the plan changed. They were going to stop at a birthday party.

Our daughter felt a little uneasy that it had not been discussed ahead of time, but since it was someone she had gone to high school with, she really did not have any trepidation. After a short time at the party, she accepted a beer and drank it. There was one man in particular who kept talking to her. He seemed nice enough, so again there was no reason to be fearful. He asked her if she would like another beer and she said yes. He brought it over to her already opened.

She had taken just a few sips out of it. Then the last thing she remembered was falling forward and landing on the floor. The next thing she remembered was waking up in the morning in the middle of a foldout couch with her pants off. She was in pain and although she had no memory of the physical attack on her, it was very apparent that she had indeed been raped. She made her way home but was so humiliated by what happened to her that she didn't tell us for a couple of weeks.

What finally gave her the courage to tell us was that she had missed a monthly period. She picked up a pregnancy test. When she took it, the test was positive. She could no longer hide what had happened to her. My heart absolutely ached for her. When she went to the hospital, now realizing that she had to get some help, I was furious at the way she was treated.

The police were called in, but because the rape happened in one town that was adjacent to another town, jurisdiction became the word of the day. A female officer had the audacity to come into the emergency room where our daughter was being treated and ask her, "Now what really happened?" Here is this 20-year-old woman who had been raped by at least one of the guys at the party, trying to get help and report a crime, and she was being treated like she was the criminal.

I cannot tell you how insanely proud I was of my daughter. In a world where abortion is as common as having a cold and at any point she could have quietly just slipped away and ended the life of this little child, instead she chose life. It made me crazy when I heard people who claimed to be Christian, who claimed to know the Lord, suggest that she would be better off if she had an abortion. They said things to her like, "No one would fault you if you ended it" or, "What is it going to feel like when you look into the face of the stranger if you have this baby?"

She never once questioned the life of her child. The only question she had during the entire time she went through the pregnancy was to ask God: "Am I supposed to be a birth mother or am I supposed to be a mother?" The woman who at the tender age of two became a diabetic and who at nine went to Lourdes, France and was filled with such a beautiful healing grace was now facing the greatest challenge of her life.

For the first few months, she was quiet. She was able to tell me how she was feeling physically, but emotionally it was still just too hard to talk about the attack. Being pregnant seemed to be very natural for her. I would see her so many times throughout the day place her hand on her abdomen, and the thoughtful way she looked was beautiful.

At the same time, she was leading music at a church in Chandler, Arizona, for a youth group. When she began to show from the pregnancy, I was so disappointed in the leadership that made her either choose to tell her story publicly or they would have someone else come in to lead music. It was way too soon to be able to talk about what had happened to her. How dare they do this to her?! It broke my heart that someone who chose life was now being penalized for it. I felt angry.

My husband, who worked for the Arizona Department of Public Safety, went to a very dark place emotionally. The very agency that was called to protect could not prevent this crime from happening. And after a number of months, they simply gave up trying to even find the perpetrators. It was like living in a slow-motion nightmare. On one occasion, we were all down at police headquarters so they could have her look through a photo lineup. I saw Kurt's deep anger. The detective in charge of the sex crimes unit made the comment that she had better be sure since rape is the most difficult case to prove and the easiest to "allege." I thought Kurt was going to lose his cool. It was horrible to feel so helpless to do something for his daughter.

With our daughter moving through this very unplanned pregnancy, being a diabetic, and needing day-to-day help, I lightened up my ministry schedule so that I was only gone two weekends a month. I felt like the best thing that I could do would be to simply support her as the baby grew and as she went through the discernment of her call to motherhood.

The day she finally heard God's answer, she had gone to Mass on a Sunday evening and while walking up to receive the precious Eucharist, she asked the Lord to give her a sign if she was to be this child's mother. As she was receiving the Eucharist, she felt the baby begin to move inside of her. She had her answer! She knew she would raise this child.

When she was telling me about it after Mass, the image stored in my heart was one of her receiving the Lord in the Eucharist, literally consuming him, becoming one with him. At the same time, the child that she was carrying in her was together with her in this incredible, intimate triune embrace. I knew that she was going to be not only fine, but amazing.

With diabetes as one of the complications in the pregnancy, it was not an easy time for her. Her blood sugars would be fine when she went to bed, but during the night they would suddenly drop so low that she would have seizures. We would hear her and try to get juice or glucose into her to bring her sugars back up to normal. At least once every other week we would have to call 911 for the paramedics to come and start an intravenous line for glucose. Kurt or I would call and then I would picture the door opening at the station and fire truck rolling out. Then in my mind's eye I would watch as they rolled to the next corner, make the right-hand turn, roll up to Greenway Road, make the left, and then 5, 4, 3, 2, 1 turn onto our street and roll to our house.

The waves of anxiety settled into a rhythm of familiarity with each of their visits. It was funny on Christmas Eve when we stopped by Station 31 after Christmas Eve Mass. We had baked a bunch of Christmas goodies and bought a couple of gifts for the regular crew there. Our gratitude for all they did for us needed to be shared with them. So, Kurt, Paul, Edel, and I brought our packages in. They were so happy to see how well Edel was feeling that evening.

Paul made the comment to them that he was 100 percent sure they would not be coming to our house that night. In fact, he said, "I guarantee you will not have to come tonight. If you do, you can wake me up to help take care of her." We went home and enjoyed a quiet Christmas Eve. Then at about two o'clock in the morning, we heard that familiar sound coming from Edel's room. I dialed 911 and within just a few minutes those bright lights were pulling up in front of our house.

The paramedic whom Paul spoke to at the station house asked, "Where is Paul's room? Get him up!" I laughed. So he repeated his question, "Where is Paul's room?" I pointed to the bedroom door at the end of the hall. He opened it, went in, and said, "Get up!" Paul jumped out of bed very disoriented, and we all started laughing. He asked why he was being woken up at this crazy hour. The paramedic said, "You promised there would be no visit here tonight. You said you were 100 percent sure there would be no visit tonight. So now you get to get up and help us with your sister."

Just a few days before Christmas, my friend Kim and I prepared a beautiful baby shower to welcome Edel's little one. We knew by now that she was having a boy. She had chosen the name Zachary Raymond for him. Zachary means "God remembers." He was my absolute bright spot in the midst of so many dark days. The new life that was growing inside of her was truly beautiful. I was amazed and overwhelmed by my daughter's courage when a friend of ours who has a public relations firm in Phoenix approached Edel and said that Fox television wanted to do a feature story about her. They wanted to focus on her bravery and what it truly means when a person says they are pro-life. She allowed them to follow her through the weeks that were left of her pregnancy, even going to an ultrasound appointment. It was like watching grace magnified every day as she stood for this precious little life.

The day after Christmas, the preeclampsia she had been diagnosed with all of a sudden progressed so rapidly that at 34 weeks she ended up in the hospital with the doctors telling her that they had to take the baby. I saw a fierceness in my daughter's eyes. It was like watching a lioness protecting her cub. She looked at me and she said, "Mom, please don't let them take him."

She was in full-blown congestive heart failure. The toxic fluid all over in her body was surrounding her heart as well, making it more and more difficult to pump properly. She made me promise that I would not allow them to take the baby even if it meant life support for her until he could be born safely.

So many people have asked me how I could agree to it. I am a mother. My daughter was a mother from the moment she had become pregnant. God in his infinite mercy took the situation into His hands when the fluid that was causing my daughter's complications also made its way into the amniotic sac. Only when the baby began to show signs of distress did Edel allow the emergency cesarean delivery to save the life of her child.

Zachary Raymond was born on December 29, 2004. He spent an entire month in the neonatal intensive care unit, NICU, before he could safely come home.

I have to be honest and share that during this pregnancy I had to go deeper than ever into prayer. When I say I went deeper into prayer, I mean I sincerely had to go deeper—reminding myself daily that prayer is taking time to talk to God and then listening to what he has to say. Besides going to daily Mass, praying the Rosary, and saying my regular daily rote prayers, I found myself inviting God into each moment of the day. When I was preparing a meal I tried to remember the way little Sister Beatrice stood next to me with her paring knife. I wanted each movement of my day to invite God closer to our home, to feel welcome there, and to stay close to each one of us. I prayed for myself, for my daughter, and for my husband. To hear her speak the way that she did of this child made my heart soar with such pride.

One of the things she said that made me know with certainty that she would be healed was when she said most women who are raped have nothing but emotional and physical scars to show for it. But in her case, she had the gift of new life. The physical scars would heal. The damage that was done to her body would be permanent; there could be no more children after this pregnancy. It only made her desire this child more. I was so proud of her. I am so proud of her.

Edel's Choice

159

Chapter 13

For me emotionally, the difficult part of the months during her pregnancy had very little to do with Edel or her unborn child. The dark part of all of this was the internal struggle that my husband was going through. The more he tried to make sense out of what happened to his daughter, the more it made him a little crazy.

One day while he was at work, he was online trying to find contact information for a friend with whom he had gone to high school. He said he was just looking to have a conversation with someone from back in the day when life wasn't so complicated. Instead of finding his buddy's information, he found the name and contact information of a woman he had dated when he was 16 years old. We will call her Risa. Within just a few clicks of the computer keyboard, Kurt and Risa were connected.

Of course, I was oblivious to what was going on for the first few months. As I said, I had pulled my schedule back so that I could be home as much as possible for our daughter and of course preparing for our grandson. There was one lovely bright spot for me personally in these months when I went to Minneapolis, Minnesota, for the UCMVA Unity Awards. I was asked to sing there. I will never forget the dates.

November 13, 2004, I was honored with the award for Artist of the Year. Earlier in 2004, I had released the recording of *The Face of God*, and it was a very special project that encourages us to see the face of God no matter what is happening around us. To see the face of God in relationships between husband and wife. To see the relationship between parent and child as given by God. To see the relationship between human beings just because we are human beings and sometimes are called to lift each other up.

I felt so happy to receive such a lovely affirmation of the work that I had been doing up to this point. The next day, I flew home to Arizona and waited at the airport for Kurt to pick me up. He was very quiet as we drove home, and as we arrived back at the house, he said, "I have to tell you something." It was November 14, and my husband asked me to go into our room so we could speak privately. He closed the door, turned, and looked at me and said, "I want a divorce."

There was no congratulations for my lovely award the day before. There was no thought of the fact that we had been married for 21 years. He simply said that he no longer wanted to be married. I was in shock. I knew that he had been growing more distant the previous couple of months, but he was also broken up over what had happened with our daughter. I figured he was trying to deal with it. I told him I was willing to go to counseling with him, but he was not interested. I asked him what was making him feel the need for a divorce, and he said he just did not want to be married to me anymore. He literally said, "There is no one else, no cookie, or anything. I just don't want to be married to you anymore."

I just broke down and wept. I couldn't understand what was happening. I felt like my life was spinning out of control. It was a long night, and it felt like morning was never going to come. I felt numb. The next day as he left for work, I went into my home office and opened my email to find my saint of the day daily reflection before going to Mass. I needed something positive to focus on.

In my email was a strange message with the subject: If Kurt Carrick from Michigan is your husband, we need to talk. Needless to say, this definitely caught my attention. I opened up the email and it was from a gentleman by the name of, we will call him Peter. In the email message was his telephone number. He just repeated the same message as the subject line when he said, "If your husband is Kurt Carrick from Michigan, would you please call me?"

I waited until I had come home from Mass and then I called him. When Peter answered the phone, I asked him how he knew my husband and all he said was, "Do you know a woman by the name of Risa from Michigan?" It was a familiar name from the past and of course I knew the name of the girl he dated back in high school. I felt sick to my stomach.

He told me that the night before she had asked him also for a divorce. I told him that we were going through some pretty rough things in 2004 and that Kurt had been in a pretty dark place for a few months. I also said something to him that I prayed would be true. I told him that I was 100 percent sure that God would take both of our families through this time and in the end we would all be okay. I promised him that I would do everything in my power to work on our marriage while he should work on their marriage.

I called my husband at work and asked him to come home early. I told him that I had had a phone call from Risa's husband. He knew that I knew. There was a lot of pain involved in this infidelity. I daresay it was more painful than what happened to us in Germany in 1988. Physical infidelity is a horrible strain on a marriage and many times feels irreparable. This time, even though Risa was in a different state, the plans that were being made for the two of them to leave their families and start over, moving even to Michigan if need be, was horrific! I felt like I had been kicked to the curb as even my in-law family was supporting his decision for divorce. In order for the divorce to be acceptable by all of them, I had become the bad guy by Kurt's telling and they believed that it was me who had changed and was no longer a good wife. It broke my heart that they no longer cared about me.

Every day just getting up and breathing seemed like an insurmountable task. Over the next month and a half, I lost 30 pounds, which I could ill afford to lose. One day, I went to the grocery store, and as I stood in front of the automatic door, it did not open. I felt like it was mocking me and affirming the fact that I was becoming invisible. In my darkest days, I felt like it would be easier if I could simply die. In complete honesty and transparency, I thought about how I could plan to end my own life and make it look like an accident. With these very dangerous thoughts going on in my head, I knew I needed some professional help.

I told Kurt that I would never go through with the divorce and that at the very least we needed some real counseling. At one point, I was having such horrible abdominal pain that I ended up in the emergency room. I'm ashamed and embarrassed to say that I was so relieved when they gave me a prescription for pain medicine; it felt like they were making it easy for me to end things. I know that my daughter saw the look in my face because when I got home she hid the bottle and told me that she would give me a dose as I needed it.

We started counseling because of my suicidal thoughts. Kurt saw one of the counselors, and I saw one of their colleagues. Elizabeth did her best to make me see what I was doing. One of the things that she told me made me angry. She said that she was going to toughen me up so that when he divorced me, I would be strong enough to stand on my own two feet.

I told her she did not understand that divorce was not an option. When we were married in the church, ours was a permanent Sacrament; we were prepared, and we knew what we were entering. There was no impediment to our marriage, and I knew that if the divorce went through, we would not be granted annulment. I would be married to my husband until death. How could we be here going through this?

I just wanted to close my eyes and not wake up. I told her that I wanted to die. She tried harder to get through to me. I remember she said that if I killed myself, I was giving permission for our son to be raised by the woman with whom my husband was having the affair. That was exactly what I needed to hear. I felt like a steel rod had been put into my very weak back. All of a sudden, I had the strength that had been missing. The thoughts of suicide literally vanished and were replaced with a fervor to live for my son and my marriage.

Every morning I went to the Word of God, where I draw real strength. I would read and pray for about half an hour before starting my daily duties and decisions. There is a beautiful prayer in the Catholic faith called the Rosary. This is an intimate form of prayer as it literally involves asking the mother of the Savior to pray with you as you look at his life and all that he was willing to do for you. The power of a mother's prayer for her children is exquisite in its grace. I needed this kind of mother's grace at this point in my life.

There are four sets of meditations, known as mysteries, and each set has five decades. There are the Joyful Mysteries, where we focus on Christ conceived in Mary's womb by the Holy Spirit, being born, presented, and found in the temple.

There are the Sorrowful Mysteries, which focus on the passion of Christ's agony in the garden, his scourging, being crowned with thorns, being crucified, and dying on the cross.

There are the Glorious Mysteries that lead us through his resurrection, ascension into heaven, sending us the Holy Spirit, then bringing His mother home to Him, and giving her the crown of her glory and queenship.

I will get to the Luminous Mysteries, or The Mysteries of Light, as they are also known. I began praying not just five decades of the Rosary, but all 20 throughout the day every single day. I was so grateful that Pope John Paul II had given us the beautiful Luminous Mysteries. I would pray those over Kurt when he would fall asleep at night. I would put my hand on his shoulder and, as he slept, I would pray the Mysteries of Light. To pray those mysteries gave me such comfort.

I would pray the first mystery, *the baptism of the Lord.* I would see our children as they were baptized, and I would find peace. When I would pray the mystery of *the wedding feast at Cana,* I began to pray not only for myself but for Risa and Peter that somehow their marriage would be spared. I'm not a saint! I was not praying because of any great desire for them to be helped, but simply because sparing their marriage would mean that she was choosing her husband over mine.

I prayed the third mystery in the beautiful words of *the proclamation of the coming of the kingdom,* that somehow that kingdom could be found in my house.

When I prayed the fourth Mystery of Light, *the Transfiguration of Christ,* God how I prayed for transfiguring grace between my husband and me. I would literally beg. I would beg Mama Mary to stand in the gap so that somehow this turmoil would turn around.

And in the fifth Luminous Mystery, *the institution of the Eucharist*, I would pray so hard that the physical presence of Christ in me and in my husband would manifest and somehow stay permanent. I know that my daughter was getting frustrated with me because I would pray a lot during the day. And she would say, why bother? He's planning on leaving. But the peace and grace I felt in prayer kept me going.

Remember my angel friend Barbara from Germany? She lives in Augusta, Georgia, and we live in Arizona. It was shortly before Thanksgiving. My phone rang and it was Barbara. She said that she and her husband were coming through Arizona and wanted to visit. No one except for my daughters, my dad, my friend Kim, and my counselor knew what was going on between Kurt and me. But I felt that Barbara was supposed to come to our home.

When she and her husband arrived, we had our pretend faces on. We didn't want anyone to know what was going on or to think badly of us. Her husband and Kurt sat down in the living room and started chatting. She took me by the hand and she said, "Show me your house." We walked down the hallway and when we walked into my and Kurt's bedroom, she turned around and closed the door and asked me to kneel down. She said: "I don't know all the details, but I know that God has sent me here to pray with you."

I wept again. For the first time, I did not feel alone. I told her what was going on and she encouraged me not to give up. She told me to continue to pray fiercely. She told me to continue to love tenderly. She said, "Don't let your heart become hard. A hardened heart cannot help anyone to heal." I am so grateful to God for my dear Barbara. There was such encouragement in the very short visit. Reminding me to pray with my husband, even if he was not wanting to, was such a gift from Barbara.

She reminded me, too, that as the bride of my husband, I needed to give myself to him physically and allow the embrace of marriage to be part of our healing. Kurt had told me he did not want to be physical because it felt like he would be cheating on Risa. That would change now. My husband, our marriage, and our gift from God could kick Satan out with the marital embrace.

I told Kurt that I could not consider divorce unless we had truly prayed first and asked God to direct us. Begrudgingly, he agreed to break open Scripture with me each morning. We would take the Bible and just let it fall open asking God what passage we should hear that day. It was such a lighthearted gift from God as we did this to find out that he does have a sense of humor. I remember that first morning just letting the Bible fall open and it landed in Ephesians. Ephesians 5:25: "For husbands, this means love your wives, just as Christ loved the church. He gave up his life for her."

He said that wasn't funny and that I should close it and let it fall open again. The second time it landed at Genesis 2:24: "Therefore a man shall leave his father and his mother and hold fast to his wife, and they shall become one flesh." Kurt thought that I had deliberately marked it to fall open to those pages and so he said, "Give me the Bible!" He allowed it to fall open as well, but it fell open to Proverbs 5, "My son, pay attention to my wisdom, listen carefully to what I know; so that you may preserve discretion and your lips may guard knowledge. Take no notice of a loose-living woman, for the lips of the adulteress drip with honey, her palate is more unctuous than oil, but in the end she is bitter as wormwood, sharp as a two-edged sword. Her feet go down to death, Sheol the goal of her steps; far from following the path of life, her course is uncertain and she does not know it. And now, son, listen to me, never deviate from what I say: set your course as far from her as possible, go nowhere near the door of her house, or she will hand over your honor to others, the years of your life to a man without pity, and strangers will batten on your property, and your produce go to the house of a stranger, and, at your ending, your body and flesh having been consumed, you will groan and exclaim, 'Alas, I hated discipline, my heart spurned all correction.'"

Needless to say, he got aggravated that he was being held to task by God. One of the other things that I asked during these months was that we would go at least once a week together to the adoration chapel at our home parish. It was the most amazing thing to go into the chapel and to kneel in the presence of Christ together. It was like we could physically feel Satan being scraped off our backs and kept outside the door when we went into the safety of Christ.

After half an hour or so, I could see light behind Kurt's eyes. We would be able to talk about real ways of working on our marriage and putting all of this behind us and moving forward. He would even consider ending this emotional affair and stopping the plans of moving away. Then as soon as we would walk out the door to go get into our car, it was like Satan was waiting there to leap back on his back. In the eight minutes it would take for us to drive home, the light would disappear and the darkness behind the eyes would be there again.

It was so painful, but each week we would go. Kurt and Risa continued making plans, and I continued to pray. Thanksgiving arrived. Each day from the time he told me that he wanted the divorce I would pray, "Lord let this be the day this ends. Let this be the day that we have a turnaround." And then I would ask Kurt is today the day that you end this so we can begin to work on us? Every day, he would say, "No, as soon as we can figure out how to do it, we will begin a new life together."

On Thanksgiving, I just knew that it would be the day of the great turnaround and we would find happiness. We did not. He did, however, help me prepare Thanksgiving dinner for the first time ever. We put on our make-believe faces and had dinner with our two adult daughters and our young son, all the while trying to keep our son ignorant of what was going on.

It continued every day with Kurt going to work while I hoped and prayed for a miracle. As I saw the ways that Satan was keeping the pressure on and attacking all that was dear to me, I felt the lioness in me get stronger. On the way to school each morning, I would say a prayer with Paul for protection and ask him to pray that God would hold him close and keep him safe in His will.

Christmas was just around the corner. I thought for sure Christmas would be the next perfect day for the turnaround. Again, it was not. It was so strange that during these months of needing to be more at home to help with our daughter as she advanced in the pregnancy, Kurt and I continued to sing for the Saturday evening Mass in our home parish each week that I was home.

How can two people who are leading music at Mass be so broken, unbeknownst to the community? These are people that we have gone to Mass with for years. We were able to put on such a good face. I was embarrassed, ashamed, and afraid to say anything to anyone outside of my counselor, my dad, and Kim. I am a Catholic recording artist and inspirational speaker. How can my life be falling down around me? What was going to happen if the marriage ends in divorce? How do I go on speaking about the love and mercy of Jesus? I know that he is constant even when we are unfaithful, but how would I go on?

And then Christmas came. And once again it was not going to be the day of the great turnaround. Our home was decorated with our pretty trees. The lights were up out front as was the lovely Nativity scene. From the outside appearance, we were a happy family celebrating the birth of Jesus. When we sang for Christmas Eve Mass I once again asked our Lord for his help. I didn't hear an answer but I did feel some peace. Four days later, on December 29, my first grandson was born. What an amazing little person! As I said before, he was born very premature because of the preeclampsia and other complications, but this little man made it! He was such a fighter. He was baptized in the NICU, and I was sure that his little life would touch the hardened heart of my husband.

Of course, we were all there at the hospital and watched in wonder as this little one was cared for so amazingly by the staff there. There's something so tender and at the same time so powerful in the NICU. There is such an amazing respect and joy in life. I was literally for the first time in months smiling from ear to ear. I felt like there was truly new life.

As we left the hospital later that night to go home, Edel was in safe hands being cared for and Zachary was here and in the best care possible. As we walked through our front door, I was still smiling and I said to my husband, "Well, Grandpa, what do you think?"

He said, "He is a beautiful little guy, but this does not change anything between us. The divorce will happen."

It was just about a week later, on January 9, that something did change. It was a Sunday morning and when I woke up something felt different inside of me that morning. As usual, I asked Kurt if today would be the day that he would make things right—if he would tell Risa that it was over and that we would begin working on us and healing. He said no once again. So, I told him that no matter what we are married. A Sacrament does not end with a civil divorce but that I could not live like this anymore.

I told him that it was now time to pack his bags and leave. I would be married to him and I would pray for him for the rest of his life, but this was just too much to continue living with. As married people, we are called to be caretakers of each other's souls, but I would have to do this at a distance. He got up and walked out of the room. He went down the hallway to get a suitcase from the closet.

As he was standing at the end of the hall, he heard a woman's voice that simply said his name. *Kurt.* At first, he thought I had called him, then he realized it was not my voice. The woman's voice continued to say *Kurt, look around you. What are you doing? Where are you going? This is your home. This is your family. What are you doing?* In that instance, he was able to see clearly with mind and heart exactly what he was doing and ultimately where it would end. It was not good. He could see the pain he had caused, and he wanted nothing more than to make things right with me.

He turned around and came back to our room where I was sitting on the bed, quietly weeping. He came in and said that he was choosing me and our marriage. He promised to end the relationship and make things right. Not knowing what had just happened with him, I did not know at first how to respond. Why now, all of a sudden, did he want to stay? Was this a trick? Why? What had changed in the 40 seconds he had been out of our room?

I didn't know if I wanted him to stay. I had finally come to accept that he was leaving. I let him hug me, but I was honestly afraid to take what he had just said seriously. I knew I had to get ready for Sunday Mass and to receive the gift of grace found there.

We went to Mass later that morning, and he just seemed to be transformed. He was kind, attentive, and sweet. He called Risa and told her it was over. The next morning, he took a day off from work and wanted to stay home.

Midmorning, the telephone in my office rang and he asked if he could answer it. When Kurt answered the phone, he heard a man speaking with a very thick Italian accent asking for Julie Carrick. Kurt asked him his name, and he responded with Fabio. He said that he was calling from Schio, Italy, and was inviting Julie Carrick to come and sing for a concert in April called Il Mondo Canta Maria, or the World Sings of Mary.

He handed me the phone and simply said, "It's Fabio, for you." I accepted the invitation graciously and told them that I would need two airline tickets and that my husband would be joining me for the trip. Can't you just feel God's sense of joy for us? And His sense of humor? I mean, Fabio? That was perfect.

It was a good 18 months before we could truly feel trust between us again as spouses. But the day-to-day desire to become close began in prayer. When Kurt realized that I had been praying the Rosary for him every day during those months of such darkness, he was only too happy to begin praying the Rosary with me every day. That daily prayer was part of our closeness and the much-needed healing that would take us past this brokenness.

We were finally able to have a conversation that began back in 1988 where those beautiful words of God were explained to us: When this couple is doing ministry together, it will be much more effective.

That morning on January 9, Kurt made the decision to join the ministry full time. On the 10th, when he answered that call, it was so beautiful that we were both invited to go to Italy and to meet this awesome community of Marian, Benedictine Catholics. When we arrived in Schio, Italy and were greeted so beautifully by the community, it was revealed to us why January 10 was the day that the invitation was made.

On November 14 the fall prior, Fabio had wanted to call. In fact, the Maximilian Kolbe radio foundation that broadcasts throughout all of Europe had a malfunction in the main studio in Schio that afternoon. They were completely off air when the main drive went down in the computerized broadcasting system.

While repairing the hard drive that runs the radio programming, he found *The Bridge* CD sitting on his desk. He loaded it to the temporary system that can play music while doing the repair. When he heard the song "Mercy," he played it over and over. Even though he speaks only Italian, he was able to understand that it was a song about falling into the ocean of God's mercy when we need it most. He did not know where the CD had come from. He asked us if November 14 was of any significance in our life.

We told him that was the day that Kurt had initially said he was filing for divorce. He told us further that every day, this entire community of 20,000 would pray for us. He said all he knew was that I was going to undergo a great sorrow and that they needed to pray for us. He did not know what the sorrow would be. And then every day they prayed, asking the intercession of our Lady

Queen of Love, as she is known there in Schio. Then each day, he would ask our Blessed Mother during prayer if he could call and invite me to the concert. Every day he heard that little interior voice spoken from Mama Mary that it was not yet time.

As he prayed on January 10, he was given the okay to call. He was assured that I would give the yes and come. We were blown away that once again the miraculous intercession of our Blessed Mother had reached us. Speaking to Kurt in our home, speaking to people on the other side of the world in a language that neither of us speak and yet praying for us this whole time. Kurt was also quite happy that Fabio looked nothing like the character on the cover of the romance novels. He was instead five feet seven inches tall with very short gray hair.

By this time, Kurt had made the decision to leave his job with the Department of Public Safety and join the ministry full time. The very first thing that we did as a couple once Kurt joined the ministry was to record the Rosary.

How to pray the Rosary
Begin with the Sign of the Cross and then
Say the "Apostles' Creed"
Say the "Our Father"
Say three "Hail Marys" one each for Faith,
Hope, and Love
Say the "Glory Be"

Announce each mystery and with each one say
the "Our Father"
Then pray ten "Hail Marys" while meditating on the Mystery
of each of the five decades of either the * Joyful, Luminous,
Sorrowful, or Glorious Mysteries.
Finish each decade with the "Glory Be" "Fatima Prayer"
After the fifth decade, say the closing prayers: the "Hail Holy
Queen" and "Final Prayer"

Apostles' Creed ~ I believe in God, the Father Almighty,
Creator of Heaven and earth;
and in Jesus Christ, His only Son Our Lord,
Who was conceived by the Holy Spirit, born of the Virgin
Mary, suffered under Pontius Pilate, was crucified, died, and
was buried.
He descended into Hell; the third day He rose again from the dead;
He ascended into Heaven, and sits at the right hand of God,
the Father Almighty; from thence He shall come to judge the
living and the dead.
I believe in the Holy Spirit, the Holy Catholic Church, the
communion of saints, the forgiveness of sins, the resurrection of
the body and life everlasting.

Our Father ~ Our Father, Who art in heaven, Hallowed be Thy
Name.
Thy Kingdom come. Thy Will be done, on earth as it is in
Heaven.
Give us this day our daily bread. And forgive us our trespasses,
as we forgive those who trespass against us.
And lead us not into temptation, but deliver us from evil.
Amen.

Hail Mary ~ Hail Mary, Full of Grace, The Lord is with thee.
Blessed art thou among women, and blessed is the fruit of thy
womb, Jesus.
Holy Mary, Mother of God, pray for us sinners now, and at the
hour of our death. Amen

Glory Be ~ Glory be to the Father, and to the Son, and to the
Holy Spirit.
As it was in the beginning, is now, and ever shall be, world
without end. Amen

Fatima Prayer ~ O my Jesus, forgive us our sins, save us from the fire of hell, lead all souls to heaven, especially those who are in most need of Thy mercy.

Hail, Holy Queen ~ Hail, Holy Queen, mother of mercy, our life, our sweetness, and our hope. To thee do we cry, poor banished children of Eve. To thee do we send up our sighs mourning and weeping in this valley of tears. Turn then, most gracious advocate, thine eyes of mercy toward us, and after this our exile show us the blessed fruit of thy womb, Jesus. O clement, O loving, O sweet Virgin Mary. Pray for us, O Holy Mother of God. That we may be made worthy of the promises of Christ.

Final Prayer ~ O God, whose only begotten Son, by His life, death, and resurrection, has purchased for us the rewards of eternal life. Grant, we beseech Thee, that by meditating on these mysteries of the most holy Rosary of the Blessed Virgin Mary, we may imitate what they contain and obtain what they promise, through the same Christ our Lord. Amen.

*The Joyful Mysteries

The Annunciation: Mary learns that she has been chosen to be the mother of Jesus.

The Visitation: Mary visits her cousin Elizabeth, the mother of John the Baptist.

The Nativity of Jesus: Jesus is born in Bethlehem.

The Presentation of Jesus in the Temple: Mary and Joseph present Jesus to the Temple.

The Finding of Jesus in the Temple: Jesus is found in the Temple discussing his faith with the teachers.

*The Luminous Mysteries

The Baptism of Jesus in the River Jordan: God proclaims that Jesus is his beloved Son.

The Wedding Feast at Cana: At Mary's request, Jesus performs his first miracle.

The Proclamation of the Kingdom of God: Jesus calls all to conversion and service to the Kingdom.

The Transfiguration of Jesus: Jesus is revealed in glory to Peter, James, and John.

The Institution of the Eucharist: Jesus offers his Body and Blood at the Last Supper.

*The Sorrowful Mysteries

The Agony in the Garden: Jesus prays in the Garden of Gethsemane on the night before he dies.

The Scourging at the Pillar: Jesus is lashed with scourging whips.

The Crowning With Thorns: Jesus is mocked and crowned with thorns.

The Carrying of the Cross: Jesus carries the cross that will be used to crucify him.

The Crucifixion and Death of Jesus: Jesus is nailed to the cross and dies.

*The Glorious Mysteries

The Resurrection: Jesus raised from the dead.

The Ascension: Jesus returns to his Father in heaven.

The Descent of the Holy Spirit on the Apostles & Mary: The Holy Spirit comes as promised by Christ.

The Assumption of Mary: At the end of her life on earth, Mary is taken body and soul into heaven.

The Coronation of Mary: Mary receives her crown of glory as Queen of Heaven and Earth.

Encouraging people every day to pray this beautiful mantra prayer of intercession is so powerful. It is not simply repeating words over and over but rather focusing on the life of Jesus Christ through the eyes of his mother. She who takes us deeper into his heart than we could ever go by our self is such an amazing maternal gift of grace. We will live every day in gratitude for the way that Mother Mary interceded on our behalf.

By the way, if you are married, we highly suggest praying this prayer by using each other's fingers. We found an intimacy in setting down the rosary beads and simply touching and gently holding each other's hands to count off the 10 Hail Marys of each decade as we pondered each mystery of Christ's life. The closeness of husband and wife in prayer is intense! I always say pray this way ONLY if you are married. It leads to the most incredible marital embrace.

Beyond the rosary, of course, you can hold hands to pray, but there is just something about slowly moving over each other's fingertips, meditating on the love of God mirrored in the life of Christ and through the heart of Mary.

Chapter 14

Then, of course, the writing continued. The lyric and the melodies went even deeper than before. To realize that there is such strength in the Sacrament of holy matrimony was grace. To realize the grace that is the part of our baptism, that stays with us and never leaves, is so empowering. To feel the grace of the Sacrament of confirmation, when we are sealed by the Holy Spirit and his word is revealed in us just like it was revealed in the prophets of old is incredible.

When we quiet ourselves and listen, God speaks to us the same way he did thousands of years ago. In the Sacrament of Reconciliation, we are absolutely restored when we get to hear that voice that the priest, who is *in persona Christi*, to be that voice of God who forgives us. That powerful grace allows transformation to happen when otherwise it couldn't happen.

In the Eucharist, the phenomenal gift of the Eucharist, we receive the intimate embrace of Jesus when he fills us with himself. For the first couple of years after Kurt had joined the ministry, we of course shared the incredible healing in our marriage. We felt like we should offer evenings of reflection and weekends of healing for couples who were struggling in their marriages.

We also knew that after that first couple of years, we were called to share about all the aspects of our Catholic faith. We had recorded a lovely Christmas record. It was really a time of celebration. It was a time of gratitude that we had been spared. We had so much for which to thank God. We had so much for which to thank our sweet Mama Mary.

After settling in and finding the new focus and rhythm in the ministry, we began again to pray together at the beginning of each year. We needed to be obedient to what God was calling us to share in this ministry. Being able to share from both a male and a female perspective was helpful for events attended by entire families.

Of course, the things that had happened in 2004 and the healing in 2005 took some time to process. As I began to write the lyric and the melodies, it was amazing how willing Kurt was to share so many of the details. Together, we came up with the idea of a new music CD that would share about every one of the Sacraments. This project, *Shades of Grace*, has a song for every one of the Sacraments.

If everyone who has been baptized would focus in on the tremendous bounty of grace in that Sacrament and remember to celebrate it, we would be so different. When we learn to cherish the gift and celebrate the reality of baptism, we will walk closer each day with Christ. Of course every one of the Sacraments is that way. Each has its own charism, or gift if you will, because each fill us with grace.

One of the songs that is so meaningful to us on that project is called "Grace." To reveal that each of us is capable of falling from grace is a reminder that we need to cling to God—a reminder that each of us, when we have failed, can turn around and run back to the wellspring from which all grace comes. Jesus is standing there waiting to love us. His love is real.

The world and so many of the things in it that are corrupted by the evil of Satan give the allure of something that they are not. There are so many evil and hurtful things in the world that look so tempting and so good, when they are in fact damaging to our eternal soul.

Working together finally with Kurt made it possible to take some of the time constraints off the ministry calendar. Our son was young enough to be able to travel with us for the summers. Kurt was no longer having to juggle between work schedule and taking care of the children if I was out of town. So I could be out of town more often, and especially when we all went together.

We took time at the beginning of each year to really ask the Holy Spirit about the direction forward. From the middle of 2005 until January 2008, we had such a wonderful time of peaceful healing and growth. We healed and grew as a couple. We found concrete ways of looking at our daily life as a married couple and making it fun again. Part of our healing process and offering that healing to others coming back from the same pain was to share what we had learned firsthand. Something as simple as the colors and textures in our home was a powerful lesson in our couple language. For example, we had lots of blue in our home. One day, when I asked Kurt what he thought about it he said, "You know, I would really like to have some of the colors I like in our home." I was shocked at this because over the years of our marriage I had specifically decorated our home with what I thought was his favorite color. He thought it was mine. Our next date was a lovely Chinese lunch and then we headed over to The Home Depot and spent some time in the paint aisle. Instead of either of us choosing things individually for our home, we started doing it together. No more "That's fine honey" or "Whatever you think is fine." By the way, we found out that we both love sage green, goldenrod yellow, and deep burgundy. Northern Italian décor is a go-to for both of us.

Our family also grew as our daughter Heidi got married and our second grandchild, sweet Dominic Vincent, was born. Family is a wonderful gift. Through joys and sorrows, we grow. Through good times and times of sadness, we grow. During times of separation, we find purpose and ultimately grow closer.

The ministry began afresh with a new vibrancy. I will be totally honest that it was a little bit strange to have been doing the ministry for 10 years alone only to have Kurt join me. I had to accept that all along it had been God's intention for us to do this ministry together. It was never supposed to have been a solo ministry. I found myself each day being more and more grateful and letting go of the little quirks that could have messed it up for us.

I know that even though Kurt allowed our journey, that was so painful and private, to become public in order to help others, it was huge for him. I don't know of too many men who would be willing to do it. The more we worked with couples, the more we saw the incredible turnaround in marriages that were ready to hit the wall. When we would do our crash-and-burn weekends, L.A.S.T. Chance (Lasting And Sustainable Transformation), as we called them, we would see more than 80 percent of marriages spared instead of ending in divorce. It was wonderful to be a part of something that was helping so many people.

We even had the opportunity to meet with Risa and Peter in Oklahoma. We were there doing an event in Tulsa and when he realized our schedule was bringing us there, he called and asked if we might be able to meet. Many times, when we would share that we had this opportunity to be able to sit down as two couples who were directly affected in such a hard way, people would get the impression that I am better than I actually am. It's not like I'm a saint who was willing to sit down and simply offer forgiveness. I'm a human being, and I have to admit part of my willingness to meet was that I was curious. Who was this person who had been receiving my husband's affections?

What was amazing was once again to see how grace was a pure gift for all four of us. We met for dinner because we agreed a public place would be best. And then after dinner, we went to their home to talk. Knowing the history gave me the compassion that I needed in order to truly offer forgiveness. When you know that someone has suffered in their life, whether by their own choosing or through circumstance, you have to learn how to be Christ for them, as we all do for each other.

I don't know if I would suggest that every couple go through this spiritual exercise, but for us it was the right thing. To be able to have four people sit down in a room, ask for and offer forgiveness, and allow the healing grace of God to give closure is one of those inexplicable gifts of the Holy Spirit. Peter had told me that they were having difficulty moving forward completely because Risa didn't believe that she had been forgiven. He, of course, told her that he forgave her, but she said if she heard it from me then she could believe that she was forgiven. I know I needed forgiveness for my own sin back when I had had feelings for my friend and I was given the incredible gift of hearing the words of Christ, spoken through Father Larry, "I absolve you, in the name of the Father and of the Son and of the Holy Spirit." Risa was a Protestant, and they did not have the Sacrament of Reconciliation and therefore didn't know about this restorative gift of grace that I had experienced so many times in my life. What finally came to me was to tell her that in a crazy way via God's grace I was grateful for what had happened. If this is what it took for Kurt to finally give in to God's desire for our ministry, then I was thankful for her presence in our life. Would I ever want to go through this kind of pain again? No! But once again it was grace that allowed something beautiful to come out of something so painful.

When I think about the gift of the Sacrament of Reconciliation, I am more grateful than ever to be Catholic. I know that people look at the Catholic Church and wonder why we have the Sacraments. There is a false understanding that we are telling our sins to the priest. As I shared my story of being a little girl who did not fully appreciate the great gift of the Sacrament of Reconciliation, I don't think many people fully understand the powerful restorative grace that comes from the Sacrament.

In the Letter of St. James, we hear Christ give us the command that when someone is ill, call the priest and He will bless us. When the soul is sick from sin, we need spiritual healing. When the priest receives the penitent, he is no longer the priest but sincerely *in persona Christi*, there in the person of Christ. Through the priesthood, he is literally there for us as Christ. We say those words out loud as we are called to confess with our lips, but when the words of grace are given to us, when Christ speaks through the priest "I absolve you in the name of the Father and of the Son and of the Holy Spirit," we answer amen because we believe that God has forgiven us.

We sat with that couple that day and were able to hear an audible asking for and offering forgiveness. God knows we are human. He gave us our senses. He knows that we need to hear the words. Can I go outside and look up into the sky and tell God I'm sorry? Of course. But he knows that I need to hear his voice. Through the priesthood, we hear the voice of Christ and we know beyond a shadow of a doubt that we are forgiven.

To be able to speak those words and to say our sins aloud is part of the healing process. We own up to what we have done, and we ask forgiveness. When we go to this beautiful Sacrament, the grace becomes more and more apparent in our daily life. One of the main reasons that I go to Reconciliation as often as I do is that if I want to be a portal of God's grace and allow the music and words that he has given me to make an impact, I have to acknowledge that I cannot give what I don't have. One of the most humbling aspects of being a recording artist, especially a Catholic one, is that I have to go deeper into this life of grace if I'm going to have anything to share. Part of being humbled was that our son, who traveled with us for a number of our summer national tours, was there to witness so much of this. As humbling as it was, I am grateful for the man he has grown up to be, a strong man of faith who has seen much and truly loves the Lord.

Grace

Lord, as I fall from grace,
help me to turn back and see Your face.
You're calling me.
Lord, when I've gone too far,
help me to turn back to where You are.
Your love is real.

Chorus: Lord God, call this broken soul.
Jesus, You can make me whole.
Your love is real.
Grace, Grace

Lord, calm this raging storm,
inside a heart that is tired and torn.
Help me heal.
Lord, take my heart of stone.
Give me a heart that's for love alone.
Your love is real. (Chorus)

In October 2007, it was such a joy for Kurt and me to host the UCMVA Unity Awards in Phoenix. He had gone through all of the work to establish a nonprofit, 501©(3) foundation to support the work of Catholic musicians and speakers. We saw so much good coming from the work that we had been doing, and he wanted more people doing this kind of work and making a difference. He saw how important it was not just for the music but for the ministry.

One of the couples we hosted that year was visiting from Canada. The gentleman had a weekly radio program where he would interview different Catholic artists and speakers. While interviewing us, he asked if it would be okay to set a first-class relic of Saint Therese of Lisieux on our table during the interview time. Relics of the saints are either first, second, or third class. First class is a tiny piece of them, that is, bone or blood fragment. Second class is a piece of something that was theirs. Third class is something that was touched by a first-class relic.

This meant having something very dear that was part of or belonged to someone who is now in heaven with the Lord. Of course, we were more than fine with having her relic in our home. Once again, we were reminded of the communion of saints who pray for us every day. We are reminded of our Blessed Mother Mary, our two boys, and the rest of those beautiful saints who have gone before us marked with the sign of faith and interceding for those of us waiting to enter eternity. It was beautiful.

The man doing our interview was married to a woman who was a convert to the Catholic faith. She said that it really bothered her that her husband had a picture of another woman hanging over his desk in his office. She was not comfortable having the first-class relic in their home either. At the end of our interview time, he asked if it would be all right for us to keep the relic permanently and keep him and his wife in our daily prayers. What a phenomenal gift to receive! As I said, this was in October 2007.

On January 2, 2008, Father Kilian McCaffrey, a dear priest friend, called and asked us about the status of our guestroom. He had recently come back from a pilgrimage to Lourdes, France. The small hotel that he and the pilgrims had stayed at was owned by a woman named Elizabeth and her brother. He mentioned to them that should they ever visit the United States, he would love to host them here in the Phoenix Valley. When she came by herself, it was obviously much more appropriate for her to stay with us than in the parish rectory. We told him that we would be happy to host her and asked when she would be arriving. He said she would be arriving on January 9.

That evening, when Father Kilian arrived with Elizabeth, we invited them in and showed her around our home where she would be staying for a few days. On a special little shelf in our dining room is the first-class relic of Saint Therese of Lisieux. When Elizabeth saw the relic, she picked it up and looked at the tiny little printing found on the front of it. She very excitedly explained that Saint Therese of Lisieux is a distant cousin of hers. What is the likelihood of a family member of this saint coming to stay in our home? It was lovely that we got to pray and have breakfast together each morning during the time that she visited here.

It's funny just when things feel like they are going smoothly and the worst is behind you, we are allowed another experience that draws us deeper into the heart of Christ. If you remember, it was January 9, 2005 that was the miraculous turnaround date for my husband and me. Now from that time forward, I don't know if Kurt actually forgave himself. It is one thing to offer forgiveness, but it is something very different to receive and accept it.

Chapter 15

When Kurt left his employment with the Department of Public Safety, our medical and other benefits changed. He secured new medical insurance for us, and it was time for annual physicals. My regular physician had moved away the previous year, so I'd not even had my regular well woman exam in 2007. I felt great, so it really did not matter much to me.

Kurt made the appointment for me and I went in to meet our new family practitioner. She was lovely. Part of the initial exam that she did included a chest x-ray. Many years prior, I had had valley fever, a lung disease caused by a fungus common in the ground around Phoenix. It left a couple of small scars in my lungs. They were no big deal but since she was now to be my new physician, she said she wanted to get a fresh x-ray just for reference.

While I was in radiology, they called her and suggested that I have a CT scan of the chest. She said I should have it done since I was already there. I went for the CT scan and then left to get some errands done. Kurt's mom and dad, who were winter snowbirds here in Arizona, were having lunch together and doing some shopping at Costco that day. We, too, had reconciled and were getting closer than ever before. I met up with them and while we were finishing our lunch, my cell phone rang.

It was the radiologist who had read the CT study of my chest. The date happened to be January 9, 2008. He was calling to let me know that he was 99 percent sure that what he was seeing in the upper right lobe of my lung was cancer. I told him that it was just scars from previous valley fever. He said he was positive that it was cancer. He went on to tell me that it looked like a very aggressive type of cancer and needed to be taken care of immediately. Of course, I would have to have a biopsy to confirm, but he did not want me to waste any time at all getting in with an oncologist and pulmonologist. I sat down on the bench in the food court and allowed a few tears to fall as I finished my call with the radiologist. My in-laws and Kurt asked me who I was talking to and what was wrong. When I rang off with him, I said those four crazy words: "I have lung cancer." Who has lunch at Costco on a Wednesday and gets a call that they have cancer?! I mean, what the heck?! We put our things we had purchased into the car and headed home. It was a lovely sunny day, the birds were singing, people were out simply being about their day and I had cancer.

I called my family practitioner, and they began trying to figure out what to do. They said it could be a matter of weeks before I could get in to see someone. I reminded them that the radiologist said it was extremely important to get in right away. It was the craziest thing that if my husband had not made the appointment for my physical, they would not have found the cancer still in a tumor stage. This type of cancer very quickly changes form into what gives the appearance of either pneumonia or some other type of infection in the lung and because of that is fatal 90 percent of the time. Normally by the time it is found, it is too late to be treated.

I was so fortunate that my friend Carole was also very good friends with the president of ICAN, the International Cancer Advocacy Network. She explained what was going on with me and that there seemed to be problems getting me into an oncology specialty right away. After speaking with her it was only a matter of hours and I had been connected with Dr. Michael Roberts, an absolutely phenomenal oncologist here in Scottsdale. The team that was put together was truly amazing.

Within a couple of days, I was in his office. After reviewing the tumor and the rest of my medical history, he told me that he wanted to speak with other specialists around the country. There was an oncologist at the Mayo Clinic in Rochester, Minnesota; Perlmutter Cancer Center in New York, New York; another one in Boston, and all I could think was that it would take time. But Dr. Roberts simply picked up his phone, spoke to his assistant, and within 10 minutes all of these specialists were on a conference call with us.

There was some talk about the possibility of different types of treatment. Radiation therapy was proposed, but it was going to destroy so much of the lung tissue that it would not work. At the time, there was not a chemotherapy that was known to treat this type of cancer. The next step would be to do the biopsy to have exact pathology so that we would know how much of my lung I would lose. From the date it was found on January 9 until March 6, we had the biopsy procedure done and went back and forth on a couple of treatment possibilities. Finally, the determination was made that I would need to have the entire upper lobe of my right lung surgically removed. The thoracotomy is a very invasive surgery. I met with the surgeon and ironically it was on March 6, my birthday. I wanted to have a little pity party, happy birthday to me.

My dear friend Karen was such a blessing in this crazy time of cancer. When I called her to tell her that I had been diagnosed with lung cancer, she was the best! She said, "What the heck?! Why do you have to be the one with cancer?" Like maybe someone else should have had it. Then she said, "Dave and I are coming down for the weekend, we are going to drink some red wine and we are going to spend some time together." They came down from Flagstaff to Scottsdale. We talked, laughed, cried, and talked about the "what ifs." Pedicures seemed like a good thing to do, too, temple maintenance and all.

The greatest lesson I learned from Karen and Dave was the strength and comfort that comes from simply being together as friends. I think that when Christ spent time with his friends, his disciples, back in the day those times of simply being together must have been the best! Scripture refers to the Sea of Galilee as the place they would go, but I have to tell you that when I was there back in 2000 I learned something lovely. The closer we got to the Galilee, I realized it was not a massive sea but simply, as the signs said, "The Lake." He went to the lake with his friends, just as Karen and Dave came to our home as friends. We simply enjoyed each other's friendship, and we did indeed enjoy some lovely red wine that weekend as well. The greatest gift to offer someone you love who is ill is simply your time. There is no need for knowing any right words to say or overthinking anything. Just be with each other and grace happens. Of course I had to write a song about this.

Red Wine

Chorus: Red wine, sharing love and living.
Red wine, bringing joy to life.
Red wine, outpouring and life giving.
Red wine, given to your friends.

At the wedding feast in Cana, a miracle occurred.
You offered joy to all who came.
The jars were filled with water, and
the blessing of Your love,
And then the water turned into red wine. (Chorus)

Along the Sea of Galilee,
a group of friends were found
sharing life and being there together.
Christ was in the midst of them
a man yet truly God
teaching them of all that's sure to come. (Chorus)

In the upper room, He broke the bread.
He lifted up the cup of wine.
By the word of Christ this simple food became
our Eternal Life. (Chorus)

With friends here in our living room
a glass of wine is shared
as we journey through this life together.
Through the joys and laughter
and through this time of tears,
the treasured gift of friendship eases fear. (Chorus)

The date that I ended up going into the hospital to have the surgery was March 20. That happened to be Holy Thursday in 2008. Holy Thursday is always the day before Good Friday during the days leading up to Easter. When I think of the way that God has constantly been present in my life, I am overwhelmed. Realizing the personal relationship that he invites us to in the Eucharist is nothing short of extreme, intimate love.

On that Thursday morning, my cell phone rang around 5:30. It was Father Kilian calling to let me know that he would like to anoint me once more before going into the hospital. I told him that his parish was quite a distance away in Mesa and that being up here in Scottsdale I would not have time to come there before going to the hospital. He said, "No, dear, I am out in my car in your driveway."

Of course, Kurt and I invited him into our home. He heard my confession, gave me the precious Sacrament of the Anointing of the Sick and the Eucharist before I went to the hospital that morning.

Again, it was Holy Thursday and the beginning of the sacred triduum of Holy Week. I never miss any of those Masses during this beautiful time of holiness. As a Catholic, this is such a powerful time of grace each and every year. It is incredibly profound to celebrate the institution of the Eucharist during the Last Supper and then to journey with Christ through Good Friday and to recall the most incredible act of love that the world has ever known. He was willing to literally suffer and die for us.

On Good Friday, I always take time to thank Christ for the incredible love that he not only said but acted upon for each of us with his death. Three o'clock is the time mentioned in sacred Scripture when he breathed his last breath. Holy Saturday is just as magnificent. It is a privilege to be there when those who are entering the church are baptized, confirmed, and received Eucharist for the first time. I never want to miss that. In fact, I have a daily alarm set on my cell phone to remind me daily at three o'clock of this most powerful gift of God's love.

But here I was heading into the hospital for quite a long time. When I arrived at the hospital, the nurse who was preparing me for the operating room asked me whether or not I had had anything to eat or drink that morning. I was not going to lie to her, so I told her that I had received the Eucharist. I explained that it was a very small host and as I continued to explain the Eucharist to her, she had me pause. She literally took her blessed scapular out from under her scrubs and showed it to me. It was a lovely blessed holy image on cloth attached by a cord that she wore every day. She then said, "Thank you for making my job easier today." She then went on to tell me that I should not tell anyone else that I had consumed the Eucharist. They do not want you to eat or drink *anything* before major surgery, and she did not want them to have to cancel or postpone my surgery that day. She knew that the Eucharist would not cause any harm to me. What a wonderful welcome that morning.

Father Kilian had also suggested to me before we went to the hospital that it might be nice if I asked my surgeon if I could bless his hands before he began the surgery. This skilled yet humble Jewish thoracic surgeon was so kind. I told him what Father Kilian had suggested and he agreed. I asked him if he could put his hands out and he did. And then I asked him if it was all right if I made the sign of the cross on his hands. I did not want to offend him since he was Jewish, but he said that no one had ever asked to bless his hands before. I explained that I am not a member of the clergy, simply a Catholic woman of faith. I told him that when my husband and I would bless our children over the years and each other, we would make the sign of the cross and ask God to bring his blessing upon them.

Again, he put his hands forward and I asked God to bless his hands, which would in turn bless me by removing the cancer from my body. It was a very touching moment to say the least. He took a few moments to look at his hands and then he said, "We are ready to do this!" He said he had never felt such a peacefulness in his life, especially with what we were about to do.

He explained that he had done the surgery hundreds of times before but never on a person who was a professional singer. My question for him was whether I would be able to sing with the entire upper lobe removed. Being that we all have multiple lobes in our lungs, breathing is not an issue even when removing multiple lobes. Singing, however, is very different breathing than regular breathing. When the hard scar tissue becomes part of the makeup of the chest cavity, it does not work the same way anymore.

He said in complete honesty that we would not really have that answer for at least six months to a year. It would completely depend on how my body would heal, and there was every possibility that I might not be able to sing again. Speaking and breathing would be fine, but singing was a big question.

One of the things that Kurt and I both wanted to do before going to the hospital for this surgery was to bring with us special prayer intentions. We were told all about the surgery ahead of time and I knew that it was going to be a very painful and slow recovery time. We did not want to waste the pain or suffering. When we think of so many people who hurt, we wanted to be able to offer up what we were going through. When I say *we*, I completely mean it. When you watch your loved one suffer, you suffer along with them. I may have had the physical pain, but Kurt had as much of the emotional pain as he watched me go through it. We sent an email to everyone in our ministry database and announced at our home church that if there were special needs they would like us to pray for in intercessory prayer, they should send them to us. Prayer intentions are always received by us in our ministry events and from folks sending them to us in the mail, via email and Facebook. We read the needs that are of real concern for people, and we lift these needs up to the Lord in our daily prayer time.

We took a small box filled with over a thousand prayer intentions with us to the hospital. I knew that when I was brought to from the main part of the surgery, I would have a spinal block in place. I was told that I would not be able to feel anything from my shoulders down. And then once the pain was more manageable, they would remove it and move me over to oral or intravenous pain medication.

When they brought me to after the surgery in the intensive care unit, Kurt was standing next to my bed. Apparently, I am one of those rare patients for whom the block did not work. He saw the look in my face, and since I was intubated, I could not talk. For those few moments I felt everything that had been cut through in my chest cavity. It was extreme pain. When they realized immediately that I was feeling everything, I was again sedated. Then they did some pain management before I was brought to again.

It was interesting that when we said we wanted to be able to *offer it up*, we were allowed to actually offer it up. What an amazing journey. On Good Friday, while still trying to get pain management accomplished, I was able to really offer something up. Seeing the look of extreme concern on Kurt's face was one of those inexplicable emotions. He was literally offering up as much as I was because he could not do anything to alleviate my pain. There was such love from my husband as he held my hand and helped me focus on my breathing while I began the healing process. Again, when I think of the incredible love and mercy of God in the way that he speaks in our life through each other, I live in constant gratitude.

One of the lovely surprises in the middle of such a difficult operation and time of healing was a visit from one of the hospital staff members. We did not know this man, but we had a mutual friend through our parish community. Our friend had asked if we were going to be at a certain hospital and I said yes but that because of the surgery I was undergoing, we were not going to be having visitors. He was very kind and simply said that he wanted to make sure I was well cared for. His friend at that hospital happened to be the CEO. He had marked my chart as a VIP patient.

Of course, we did not know this beforehand. It was when he was visiting in our room to ensure that everything was good for me that he revealed who he was. Everyone who cared for me during my stay treated me with the utmost care, and I felt like I was someone very special.

The pathology report came back on Monday afternoon. All of the cancer had been contained in that lobe. The lymph nodes were clear. Thanks be to God, all I had to do now was heal. I began the breathing and physical therapy that would be part of my healing process while in the hospital.

I can still see my mom's and dad's faces as they spent time with me at the hospital. My mom stayed overnight one of the nights to make sure her "little girl" was being well cared for. Heidi also stayed overnight with me one of the nights. Having her there with me was such a gift of healing love. Mother-daughter relationships seem to undergo tests unlike any other relationship known to humankind. I think the reason emotions are so deeply felt is that the love goes so deep. All I can say is that I was blessed to have had both of my daughters near me during this time of my life. On Easter Sunday, which also happened to be my daughter Heidi's birthday, my whole family came to the hospital to visit and celebrate our risen Lord. Of course, for me it was very quiet but so incredibly beautiful to have my daughters and grandsons there.

I was able to leave the hospital a week later. It was on Saturday morning and I was home in time for Divine Mercy Sunday. I had been scheduled to sing for Divine Mercy Sunday along with Kurt up in Williams, Arizona. But my daughter Edel went in my place. She was able to share her beautiful voice and be a living witness to God's mercy in her life and in the life of her son, Zachary. Heidi stayed at home to take care of me. My daughters lovingly cared for their mama, each in their own way.

Life was turned around and yet the lovely grace pouring through my family was so divinely gifted I could not be anything but hopeful. It was the first realization that I was going to have to learn how to wait with patience. The schedule that had been planned for 2008 included a national ground tour. We were scheduled to do concerts in New Mexico, Texas, Missouri, Ohio, and many other states. With the diagnosis of the cancer and the eventual thoracotomy, we had no choice but to cancel that tour.

The doctors told me that I needed to be patient and continue to do the breathing exercises and physical therapy. Six months to a year seemed like a very long time.

The support for us personally and through our ministry was overwhelming. We could not have been more blessed. At least that is what we thought. God in his mercy did not make us wait a year or six months for the answer as to whether or not I would continue singing. It was on the feast of Corpus Christi, the body and blood of our Lord, that my voice was not only restored but expanded. My range increased by three additional notes, two higher and one lower. Three full octaves! It was amazing!

Being that the Rosary was a part of my daily prayer life, I asked Mary to continue to journey with me during this time. In addition to prayer, I was constantly pondering the life of Christ through the heart and life of his mother. I knew there was one song about her that was very special to me. When I was able to sing it, that would be the proof for me that it was time to get back to work. The song that I wanted to be able to sing again someday was "Gounod Ave Maria." When that happened within just a matter of weeks after coming home, I was to the moon! I was so grateful to God that he was going to allow me to continue to serve Him through the gift of voice.

Chapter 16

Kurt and I realized that we would indeed be able to do at least part of the national tour after all. We called a number of the parishes that had been originally scheduled to see if they still wanted the events. They did. The only stipulation from my medical team was that at the halfway point of the tour, I was supposed to take a week off and just rest. I was so excited!

We had received a gift of a Class C motorhome that we could use for the tour. Since I was not able to fly yet, this was the perfect answer. The midway point of the tour was in Ohio. With my brother Eugene's permission, I would like to share some of that story.

When I called him and said we had a motorhome to use and that we would be taking a week off in Ohio, I wondered if he knew of an RV park near his home. He said better than an RV park, we could literally stay on his property where he had just put in a 50-amp service.

His wife, Gwen, is such a sweetheart! She was overjoyed when she realized that we were going to be able to spend a week together. She used to yell at me when I would come and do events in Ohio. I would only spend a day or so with them in between the parish work. She said that an entire week was an absolute gift.

We left Arizona in June and by the first week of July, we had done quite a few concerts and parish missions and were now ready for our time off with family. I was already beginning to learn a lesson in finding something good coming out of cancer. It was teaching me to slow down and live in the moment. I was grateful for the gift that was now giving me a week with my brother and sister-in-law.

Our son, Paul, was so fun on that trip as well. Aunt Gwen took us to a county fair. They had little rides set up in the center of this little town, and she made sure that Paul had a wrist bracelet so he could ride on every one of them. He was terrified because he said they did not look safe, but he went on most of them anyway. We visited and talked and laughed and had the most wonderful time together. That was on Monday.

On Tuesday evening after dinner, Gwen suggested that we have a family movie night. She had a movie ready along with popcorn and other snacks and drinks. She wanted us to watch *The Bucket List*. We sat together as a family and watched a movie that really made us take a look at our lives. What was important to us? How would we spend precious time if we knew we had a short time left to live? At the end of the movie, Gwen told us that if she knew she had only a small time left to live, she would not want to climb mountains or drink crazy coffee. She said this, spending time together as family, was most important to her.

That evening, we took a walk and we shared things we never had the opportunity to share before. I told her that I was so glad that she is my brother's wife and that she is a wonderful wife and friend. On Wednesday evening that week, my brother was working a second shift and was at work when we had finished dinner and were sitting in the living room together.

All of a sudden, Gwen leaned over in her chair, grabbed her chest, and started crying out that she was in pain. Kurt had been trained well when he worked for the Department of Public Safety, Highway Patrol, and he knew immediately that she was having a heart attack. She was only 55 years old. He told me to call 911, and he worked on her until the paramedics arrived.

It was amazing that we were there with her when she needed us most. They were able to successfully transport her to the Cleveland Clinic, a cardiovascular center. I rode in the ambulance with Gwen. Kurt and Paul followed in the car. Meanwhile, they called my brother Eugene and told him to meet us at the hospital.

By the time the cardiologist came in with what he felt was a diagnosis, he said he thought it was not a heart attack but something else. He said he wanted to keep her for a couple of days to run some tests to be sure, and we were relieved beyond words. On Thursday, they ran a bunch of tests and everything was looking okay. We took her shoes home with us because she was joking around that she was going to sneak out that afternoon and come home. She really didn't like being in the hospital. On Friday morning, we were supposed to go and pick her up and bring her home. But they called and said we should come in right away as she had taken a bad turn during the night.

By the time we arrived at the hospital, we were greeted at the door and taken to a private waiting room. The cardiologist who had seen her in the emergency room came in and said the words that no one wants to hear. He said, "I am sorry. We did everything we could, but she did not make it." She died in the catheterization laboratory while they were trying to clear a blockage. It had indeed been a heart attack on Wednesday evening. Her heart was too weak to start again once they had cleared the problem. I will never forget the look on my brother's face as he tenderly touched Gwen's face, kissed her goodbye, took his scapular off, and gently laid it over her shoulders and then sobbed. Paul stood next to his Uncle Eugene and silently let his tears fall. After some time, we all hugged each other and made our way back to their home to begin the preparations for her funeral.

It is crazy, isn't it? When we look at so many of the situations in life, why do they happen like they do? Why would God slow me down enough that we would literally be with Gwen so that Kurt could take care of her and get her to the best heart hospital in the country only to let her die? The real answer is this, God knew the exact day that Gwen would come home to him. He also knew that Eugene would not be able to take it if he came home and found her deceased. He knew that we would be there together as family to prepare her funeral and to be there with my brother when he needed us most.

Did God give me cancer? No. Did he know that I would have it? Yes, he did. When we begin to offer God everything, and I mean everything, we begin to see things differently. I would never want to go through the pain of infidelity again. I don't relish the thought of ever going through a thoracotomy again either. But what we began to learn by living through these hard experiences is that when we can offer everything into the mercy of God, life begins to have purpose. We can't truly have empathy for anyone until we have had the experiences that allow us to connect in real ways.

Christ took on human flesh so that we would be able to literally take him at his word. He came and suffered for us. He came and made a difference in this world by literally giving his life for us. When we can learn to embrace our sufferings and ask God to reveal the purpose, we grow so much in our faith.

Up to this point in life, I've shared with you some beautiful joys—marriage, growing a family, living in beautiful places of the world, and having a family grow stronger. I've also shared some of the darkest days of my life. It is so painful to lose children in infancy. It is so painful to suffer relationship pain, and it is hard to deal with illness. But the grace that comes out of all of it is that the more we can unite our suffering to the suffering of Christ, the closer we come to his Sacred Heart.

Watching my brother journey through the loss of his wife made me embrace my life with Kurt all the more. I do not take one day for granted. I know that tomorrow is not promised to any one of us, and so we live in the grace of today. The hardest part of suffering and going through things that are difficult is waiting.

One of the beautiful gifts that I received during this time of illness and then during the loss of my sister-in-law was the most beautiful poem written by my cousin's wife. Her name is Cindy. When I received the treasure of her poetry, it affected me deeply and I realized that there were ways that her gift and my talent of song could work together to bring this gift of grace to so many people. And yes, once again, a beautiful recorded project would be the fruit of so much suffering.

My dear friend Judy during this time of writing new songs was diagnosed and went through treatment of breast cancer. Watching her battle bravely strengthened my resolve to make the new project more meaningful and prayerful than any other project I had done. One defining writing day was when I took a break from writing melodies to go with her to the salon so we could have our hair shaved off super short. She was about to start chemotherapy after all the radiation treatments. The doctors told her she would lose all her beautiful long hair. She had journeyed with me through lung cancer, and now I would journey with her.

As I finished writing the songs and pulled together music that fit this theme of finding purpose in the waiting, I was able to thank God every day for allowing this journey. When it was time to go into the studio, I realized that the person whom I had worked with previously as my producer could not do this project. For a number of personal reasons, I just could not work with him on this one.

At the same time, my friend Rick Elias had come back into my life after a few years apart. We toured together after Rich Mullins passed away many years ago. Rick produced the *Jesus* record, and I loved it! He also produced a number of other records and when he approached me about the possibility of recording this new record in Brentwood, Tennessee, I just knew that it was a God thing.

I mentioned Gary Lunn very early in the book. I love the way that God brings things around full circle. Remember the way that I was describing tapestry earlier? Rick, Gary, Janice, Rhett, Barbara, and so many other beautiful people are the lovely threads that make up the strength and beauty of the tapestry in my life.

So many years prior, when I had been sponsored by Pepsi to go to Nashville and record that first record, Gary Lunn played bass on the project. Now it was 2011, after going through so many life experiences and meeting so many people that God had introduced into my life for so many reasons, and here we were.

Rick had scheduled the recording session to be at Sunset Blvd Studios in Brentwood, Tennessee. When I arrived on the second day of the session, the band members who were going to be playing the primary tracks were already there tuning and warming up. When I came into the studio, Rick introduced everyone by first name only: Jason, Dave, Brew, and Gary.

We had just listened through the rough of the first song, "In the Waiting," when Gary looked up and asked, "Did we work together on a project back in the late '90s?"

I thought his face was familiar. I said, "Yes, I believe we did." Bob Metzger had put a group together to record for that project.

Back in 1997, the group of musicians hired for that project was not happy about what was happening. It was day after day playing music on very mediocre songs that were quite frankly a money grab, and they were tired of it. People were promised all kinds of record deals where only a small number were making money. These very talented session players were being paid to make beautiful music out of songs that really should never have seen the light of day. I was there recording for the project that Pepsi had sponsored, but there were a variety of others. These very talented musicians were tired and quite frankly angry about what was going on behind the scenes.

What I didn't know was that at the point that I heard my songs come to life, Gary had reached a point where he was ready to walk out. He came into the hallway and, unbeknownst to me, saw me crying. When he approached me, and I was able to thank him profusely for the beauty with which my music was coming to life, he looked shocked.

We realized in retrospect that we both reached a turning point at that time. He very well could have stopped doing music, and I may have never started if it had not been for that work done together in Nashville. Once again, I was able to see how grace had poured into my life as well as Gary's. He was so surprised that someone would thank him and acknowledge his part in making such beautiful music.

And now all these years later, God allowed me the gift of hearing his lyrics and melodies. These songs have touched so many hearts over the years. It was one of those moments where it felt like time stood still. The band members were looking at us and we were trying to figure out how to share such a profound story of grace. It literally took years to fully understand just how much God had woven together our lives. Each time a new project has been recorded, I have been so grateful that Gary and those talented like him are willing to work together to allow the beauty of God's love to come through in music that opens the soul to receive such grace.

This new project, *In the Waiting*, would be comprised of songs that help people find purpose in suffering. The songs were intended to show us that we can bring this suffering to the cross and lay it at the foot of Jesus. In this way, we come closer to his Sacred Heart. There is a profound grace that can transform us when instead of becoming bitter and angry over suffering, we can find its purpose by offering it up and growing from it. Gary's lovely wife, June, allowed me to include her beautiful photo in the video portion of the new project as a cancer survivor. She, like so many, have had multiple bouts of illness, but continue to love the Lord and live in His grace. It was the most beautiful thing to realize that God had allowed one more thing in my life to come full circle.

In The Waiting

Here in the waiting, I'm scared. I do not want to give in to despair.
Help me cope, help me hope, past the doubt, lift me out.

Chorus: Lord, I call to You. Help me make it through.
Jesus, take my hand, help me understand.

Here in the waiting I've found, your love is holding me,
keeping me calm
through the fears, through the tears, past the pain, God You reign.
(Chorus)

Here in the waiting, I know all will be well as this story unfolds.
By this grace, by this faith, Jesus Christ, You are life.

Final Refrain: Lord, I call to You, help me make it through.
Jesus, hold my heart, I choose the better part.
Jesus, take my hand, help me understand.
Lord, I called to You. With You I've made it through.

Once again, something that could have been taken for granted had a larger purpose in God's plan. As a recording artist, you bring music as part of the presentation. It's easy to see how it could become about the music. I know that I am known for music, but the life experiences that make up the fabric of our common journey are so much more important. And yet without the music, the emotional attachment is so often missing. We can never take anyone for granted.

Chapter 17

It's been an interesting journey. Since 2011, each of the projects that I've written and recorded have come together at Sunset Blvd Studios. Again, that is not a coincidence with God. He knew that Gary and I would reconnect and be able to tell each other thank you for the impact from all of those years prior. Just as it was not a coincidence that the projects that were recorded at the Gaither Studios were recorded there. To be able to share my Catholic faith with these beautiful, humble-hearted people who are so talented and gifted was not a coincidence. To be able to share the beauty of my faith and to be able to learn from the experiences of those people that God has brought such beauty from for my music is a gift of grace.

I wish I could say that every circumstance has ended on an up note, but all we can do is plant the seeds and allow God to tend the garden. The majority of the folks who have spent time with us since Kurt joined the ministry have learned from our pain and suffering and realized that life can be something more beautiful than what it was in the midst of darkness. Then there are those

225

hardened hearts that will not accept the gift of grace, and the best and most that we can do is to pray for them.

More than once, I mentioned the adoration chapel. I want to tell you just how magnificent and powerful and tender the visit with Jesus can be here. So many people around the globe in every language under the sun go and visit with Jesus in the most holy Sacrament, the Eucharist. They spend time there in prayer and supplication to him. They spend time loving him. But to really explain what happens there, I need to share one of the most important lessons I learned about spending time with Jesus.

Remember how Father J.T. so pointedly helped me realize that I needed to just be with Jesus and not be so busy with him? The beauty of the songs that have come from the way that I spend time with Jesus is just perfect. Well in 2012, just when I thought I couldn't possibly go any further in my understanding of this amazing gift from God, he plunged me further into the depth of his love.

Kurt and I were doing a parish mission at Immaculate Conception Catholic Church in North Little Rock, Arkansas. Prior to going in to begin, we had the opportunity of a private hour of Eucharistic adoration in the chapel. That day, as I looked into the little window of the monstrance that held Jesus's precious body, I heard his voice. It was different than the way I normally hear him when he is speaking the lyric and melodies in my heart. It was different than when I hear him tenderly soothe my anxious heart when I am concerned for a loved one. That day, I heard his voice much more audibly, more like he was speaking in the room than internally like most of my visits. As I looked into his face I heard, "Julie, this is not a one-way glass. You are not just looking at me, I am looking at you and I love you." I began weeping. I didn't know why the tears were streaming down my face. I felt like a floodgate had opened up and every emotion I had ever felt was flowing down my face. In an instant, I felt his pure love for me as much as I felt a loathing of myself for the way I had always come to adore him.

Up to that day, though not on purpose, I had come very arrogantly to be with Jesus. What I mean by this is that I would look at my busy calendar and find a time that I could spare to set aside and come to give that time to Jesus. Oh, my God! When I heard his tender loving voice that day, I guess I realized that I had been arrogant. The tears flowed out of the extreme gratitude that my heart and soul were realizing in that instant. The King of kings, Lord God Almighty was there waiting to spend time with me and love me and I bothered to show up. I felt so unworthy and I told him so. I just wanted to offer him perfect praise. I wanted to give him all of me and not the attitude that I was somehow doing something for him, when he was the one giving me everything I need for this life and eternity. I wanted to receive him into my heart. I begged him to never let me take for granted the gift of being able to look at him face-to-face.

I acknowledged that every breath was a gift, and I longed for his embrace. I could see the unworthiness of myself and almost felt like I needed to get up and out of that chapel. But his gentle love held me there. I began to hear a melody and once again the beauty of lyric forming inside of my heart, and the song he gave me that day has become one of invitation for everyone to come to him.

Adoration

I come to offer perfect praise to You, to bring a gift of "self"
to offer. Kneeling here before You now, I feel unworthy, Lord.
Help me lift my eyes to see, to see You looking into me…

Into a heart that longs to love You, into these eyes that beg to see,
into my arms that need Your true embrace. Into my hearing,
all my senses, into every breath I breathe, Jesus, Jesus.

My soul is longing to be near You, I see beyond the
bread your face.
Kneeling here before You now, I wonder in the awe,
The God of life and grace, I see you looking into me…
Into a heart that longs to love You, into these eyes that beg to see,
into my arms that need Your true embrace. Into my hearing,
all my senses, into every breath I breathe, Jesus, Jesus.

Oh Lord, how can it be, that You can love me so?
Your presence fills this place and my soul.
Oh Lord, how can it be, that You would give your life for me?
I thank You, Lord. I praise you, Lord. I love you, Lord.

This gift of love that I now offer is the gift of love first come from
You. Kneeling here before You, Lord, I know this truth divine.
You have set me free as you are looking into me…

Into a heart that longs to love You, into these eyes that beg to see,
into my arms that know Your true embrace. Into my hearing, all my
senses, into every breath I breathe, Jesus, Jesus. Jesus, Jesus.

I could so easily see how Satan would use the feeling of unworthiness to make me feel like I am not suitable to be in the presence of Christ. Yet it is Christ himself who invites us to come to him! No one on earth is worthy to come into the presence of God, but his love and invitation makes us worthy to receive his gift of grace.

This beautiful visual "veil," if you will, allows us to see God face-to-face and not literally explode. In Exodus chapter 33, when Moses had the encounter with God, he was changed. In this Scripture, it says no one may see the face of God and live. In fact, Moses was only allowed to see the back of God after his glory had passed.

Christ, however, offers us the gift of himself fully present but under the appearance of bread. Our soul knows and is transformed just as Moses was transformed in the presence of God. You can call a Catholic church near you and ask whether they have an adoration chapel or when they have specific times to experience this extreme gift from Christ. Lord, may my mind become still in your presence to hear you. Be still, my heart, and experience the embrace of our Lord.

Chapter 18

One of the absolute privileges of these years of ministry is that in every parish mission concert or conference, we ask people for their prayer intentions. These little slips of paper, where people write their needs and their pains down, come with us into our daily prayer. I love it, too, when folks write down their prayers of gratitude. We have a little wooden box that is shaped like a book. I love how at the end of each tour or event, we take all of these little slips of paper, put them in there, and then take that box to the adoration chapel and kneel down in front of Christ to offer them into his grace. It is such a privilege.

Over the years of doing this ministry, it would be easy to have the scale tip in the direction of either extreme. When I see some of my contemporaries who are famous recording artists, it would be easy to feel jealous. Wouldn't it be wonderful to sing in the giant arenas and be driven there in limousines? Wouldn't it be wonderful to be paid $50,000 for every event that I do? Wouldn't it be wonderful that radio networks who claim to be Christian would play my music along with other Christian artists?

That's not what it's about. It is about realizing the powerful gift of grace in real life. Whether we are recording artists or mailmen, whether we are nurses or teachers, whether we are chefs or dishwashers, what matters is that each and every moment of our day we find the reality of God's grace and live in it. For whatever reason, God has allowed a large number of trials in my life, but when I look at the phenomenal numbers of miracles, I will live every day of the rest of my life in gratitude. I honestly believe that if every person would approach each day with an openness to God's grace, we us would see so much more grace than darkness. We just need to be open to it.

I trust those relationships with Christ in the Eucharist and with his mother are the main portals of grace and why I believe I am still here today. There is a lovely saying in daily life of many Christians, "Jesus Christ is my personal Lord and Savior." I believe that with every fiber of my being.

The joy for me as a Catholic, however, is that the intimacy of that personal relationship is experienced in the Eucharist. When I think of the words of Jesus Christ in John 6:35–66, we hear Christ give us the full knowledge of who he is in the Eucharist. He says it over nine times that his body is truly our food and His blood is truly our drink. The line that gives me the absolute proof is verse 53 when he says, "Unless you eat the flesh of the Son of Man and drink his blood you do not have life within you." I need him in me for life.

I know that in the Catholic faith, we know that we belong to Jesus when we are connected to the roots of our faith. He gave us the Catholic faith. Is it perfect? No. Are her teachings perfect? Yes. The teachings of Christ in her have never failed. People involved with it over the years have failed, of course. We are human beings. But to throw away or change the teachings of the faith just because some humans have failed is not right.

To break away or to protest the teachings of the Catholic faith given to us by Christ removes us from the Eucharist. I never want to be removed from the Eucharist. When I am at Mass and I fully participate and hear the word of God given to us, I am completely fed. For the first 387 years of Christianity, Mass was how the first disciples participated in the faith founded by Jesus Christ. Even now, it is a reminder that we are literally participating in that paschal mystery.

What so many people do not understand about the Mass is that it is not a re-creation of anything. It is the same Last Supper that happened in the upper room when Jesus took the bread and broke it, took the chalice of wine and gave it. He told his apostles, "This is my body given for you. Do this in remembrance of me." And then it was not just his word that was spoken in Capernaum, as we read in John 6, but the manifestation of his word given in the Last Supper. That alone didn't fulfill his word, however. What fulfilled his word was literally going through the crucifixion, death, and resurrection.

The intimate relationship that he wants with each of us, to be our Lord and our Savior, was fully manifested when he embraced the crucifixion. He knew where he was headed, and every day it brought him closer to Jerusalem and the triumphant entrance that we celebrate on Palm Sunday. Every day, he drew closer to embracing the greatest act of love that the world would ever see. He gave himself in ransom for our sins; that is truly a personal relationship with Christ.

To claim him as Lord and Savior is one thing, but to humble ourselves and be obedient to his teaching is something else. It's not easy to be Catholic. I remember back in the day going to Nashville on a regular basis when I was a member of the Gospel Music Association. I was treated differently because I was Catholic.

After releasing the *Kateri* record in 2000, I was approached by one of the major labels in Nashville. It was that phone call that all recording artists want to receive. They were offering me, not a single, but a three record deal. I told them that my family recently moved to the Valley just a couple years prior. I was not open to moving to Nashville, but I would maintain an address there if need be.

We worked through the details of what I was willing and unwilling to do, what they were willing and unwilling to do. I remembered the words of Rich Mullins cautioning me about what was a good idea and what wasn't. I could hear the echo of his voice reminding me not to be indebted to a label but be willing to work hard.

The day finally came to fly there, sign a contract, and get to work. I was excited to arrive at the A&R office and sit down with the executives. When they handed me the contract, I looked over the front and everything seemed to be in order as we had discussed. I turned through the couple of simple straightforward pages, and it wasn't until the last page that I saw the three addendums.

The first one was that I was supposed to be blonde. I kind of laughed until I looked up and saw that they were serious. The second item was ridiculous! I was supposed to agree to a breast augmentation, on their dime. How ridiculous that physical appearance was more important than what I was supposed to be there doing as a Christian artist.

The third one was reprehensible. It was literally a gag order stating that I was not allowed to tell anyone that I was Catholic while I was under contract. In hindsight, I realize that the first two were most likely the ones that they would have been willing to give in on if I relented on the third provision. What was crazy was that to this point, the broad term *Christian* was acceptable by radio stations and by large entities around the country. For some reason, being Catholic was a no-no.

I asked them what their problem was with me being Catholic. They said they could not have someone who belonged to the whore of Babylon represented by their label. Clearly, they have no understanding of the Catholic faith. They tried over the next few minutes to make me understand their interpretation or belief of the Catholic Church, and there was no way that I was going to accept those distorted ideas.

At one point, they tried convincing me that I would no longer have to sing in little churches, only in large arenas and my

Christian message would reach many more people that way. They really tried to color it so that I could accept denouncing my faith. The next crazy thing was at that point they slid a check across the table in the amount of $250,000. In the memo attached, it stated that this money was not in any way to be recouped by the label; it was simply a bonus. No strings attached.

I told them that if I accepted their check and signed this contract, I would indeed be a whore. I would be doing it for money instead of the honor and glory of God. I have never regretted my decision. When I think of the beauty of the Eucharist and the fact that for the first 387 years of Christian life, Mass was celebrated every day with those first apostles and disciples, those men who shared Christianity with the known world, I am grateful I belong.

When the Bible was fully complete 388 years after the beginning of the Christian church, it does my heart good to know that I belong to the faith that brought the word of God as the Bible to the known world. I think of those beautiful monks and priests who kept the word safe and listened and were inspired by God to compile what we know as the Bible.

Just as there have been problems in the Catholic church because of human folly, so there have been problems with every religion on the planet. My prayer is that each time I do an event, meet someone, or allow another thread in this tapestry of life to be included that I can share a little bit more about the reality of the Catholic faith. I sincerely hope that somehow and someday we will all be under one roof again receiving Christ in the entirety of who He is in the Eucharist.

Chapter 19

O ne of my favorite projects as an artist is the CD *I Take You at Your Word*. It is about the beauty of Jesus Christ in the Eucharist, our Lord and Savior intimately uniting with us. It's such a privilege and such a joy.

One of the other areas of the Catholic faith that is so misunderstood is the life of Mama Mary. When I think of this incredible woman who has stood in the gap so many times in my life, I am absolutely overwhelmed. I think of that little girl in Free Soil, Michigan, who joined the sodality group just so that I could get closer to Jesus. That's what Mary offers every person.

One of the words in Scripture that transformed the way that I look at her comes from Luke's Gospel. It is simply the word *conceived*. A few years ago, when I was reading through that Scripture, I was also reading a book by Father Michael Gaitley, *33 Days to Morning Glory*. Once again, it was no coincidence that I had been asked to do an event in St. Louis, Missouri for a parish that was doing a consecration exercise. They wanted a Marian concert to celebrate its culmination.

When my husband scheduled the event, I asked him to tell me a little more about it so that I could be prepared. He said that they were doing a study about Mary, and it was a 33-day preparation for Marian consecration. I thought they probably wanted more than a concert.

Many years prior, I studied the life of Saint Louis de Montfort. He had a beautiful way of looking at the life of Mary, but honestly, it was a little hard to take. Most of us find it hard to let someone help us when we want to do everything by ourselves. That was how I used to feel about my relationship between Mary and Jesus. I felt like I did not *need* her to take me closer to Jesus. I loved having her in my life, but I could go to Jesus by myself, thank you just the same. She was more of a stepping-stone kind of helper.

And here it was time to revisit this area of consecration. I learned from this parish about Father Gaitley, his *33 Days to Morning Glory* study about Mary, and what it means to be consecrated through her. I also told Kurt that if I was going to read this and use it to prepare for the event, then I wanted him to do it with me. We each bought our copy of the book and began our 33-day study.

What was so different this time was that instead of looking at one person's idea, namely Saint Louis de Montfort, he showed us how to look through the eyes of other people. The other people who Father Gaitley shared with us were Saint Maximilian Kolbe, Mother Teresa of Calcutta, and Pope John Paul II. To look at the way they journeyed through life, asking Mama Mary to intercede for them, was transformative. The more I saw her through their eyes, the more I wanted to go deeper in my understanding of her and my love for her.

The misunderstanding that is so prevalent in the world about Catholics and Mary is that there is a belief that we worship Mary. I will make it very clear, we do not worship Mary. We honor her because God honored her. But we do not worship her. Worship is for God alone.

But that word, *conceived*, kept poking at me. Every time I would go to the adoration chapel during that 33-day period of prayer, I would hear Jesus inviting me, almost directing me, to write music about his mama. I let that kind of resonate in the form of doing a Marian-focused music project. I thought to myself that "Ave Maria" would be a good song to record. There are others, written by so many musicians, like "Hail Mary Gentle Woman," that could together make a nice record.

But that was not what her son wanted. Jesus was literally giving me a song a day for those 33 days. I was absolutely blown away by the depth of the lyric and the beauty of the melodies. It was crazy! I had no intentions of writing any music or doing a record, and before I knew it 33 days had passed, and the songs were amazing.

Again, that word *conceived*. Let your mind wrap around it for a minute. In Luke's Gospel we read that passage, "and she conceived of the Holy Spirit." It was not divine in vitro fertilization, right? It was not like baby Jesus already was an infant and just placed inside of her when the Holy Spirit overshadowed her. Mary, who is known in one of her titles as the spouse of the Holy Spirit, had the most intimate union we can have as human beings. And she had that union by literally conceiving Christ in her womb. That blew my mind.

I have been a cradle Catholic and have lived this faith my whole life. I have, in so many ways, been kept safe in the womb of mother church despite so many trials, temptations, and tribulations in my life, and I came to this realization through one word. How can we not love Mary? How could we not honor her? She is literally, physically, the mother of Jesus Christ.

I started looking at her life in a deeper way. I realized that at a tender young age, she was approached by the angel Gabriel and was able to affirm her complete faith in God, because she had a deep personal relationship with him. She was betrothed to Joseph and yet was willing to become pregnant, knowing that if Joseph put her out and said that child was not his, she would be stoned to death. She said yes despite it all.

We know that Mary was presented in the temple, which means she would have had a basic knowledge of the prophets' teachings. They foretold a virgin birth and here she was being asked to be the mother of Christ. She said yes! Then, after saying yes never lost heart, never lost faith in God no matter what trial or tribulation she experienced. Here she was, a teenager pregnant by God on the back of a donkey going to Bethlehem with Joseph out of obedience. Having given birth three times in my life, I can assure you it was complete obedience on her part to travel at that point in her pregnancy, and on a donkey nonetheless!

What does Mary teach us? She teaches obedience to give our yes and to live that yes. They found themselves in Bethlehem and instead of the comfort of an inn, there was no room for them. So where did they end up? In a barn. Don't you just love how the Christmas cards and carols sentimentalize all of it and make it sound so lovely? But it was a barn! But even that had such purpose when we realize that through the eyes of Mary, through the life of Mary, we are already learning in his infancy that Jesus will become our very sustenance in the Eucharist. She laid him in the manger. The word manger in Latin is *manducate* (manducare). The literal translation of that word means *take and eat*. To literally consume! Mary, who carried the Christ in the first place, next laid him in the manger. This is the foreshadowing the Eucharist.

What happened next? The shepherds came and adored. The angels sang the praises of God as he was born. Imagine the euphoric sense of joy and pride that Mary must have had seeing these things unfold before her. And then the kings came in. They brought gifts, but these weren't ordinary gifts. The gift of gold represented his kingship. Frankincense represented the beautiful lifting up of prayer and indicated that he would be an offering. Myrrh represented the sorrow of the burial ointments. Why would you bring burial ointments for an infant baby? All of these gifts were laid out in front of her.

Then they had to flee into Egypt. At any point along the way, Mary could have thought that she was being used by God, but we know that is not the case. She could have been upset or angry, but she wasn't. Herod called for the life of every male child under the age of three and in order for her son to be spared, obediently she went away until it was safe to come home.

And then when it was finally time for them to bring Jesus and present him in the temple, there was another shock for Mary. Simeon spoke those words that initially were such a joy to her heart. He exclaimed that God could literally take him because he had seen the fulfillment of the promise of the coming of the Savior. Then he looked at Mary and said, "You woman, a sword of sorrow will pierce your heart."

Mary was young, of course, but she was no fool and no puppet. There were many things that were revealed in the life of Christ. As they were revealed, they went deeper and deeper into Mary's heart. Again, in the words of Saint Luke, Mary pondered and held all of these things in her heart. Psalm 22, which is one of the psalms prayed in the Jewish community, foretold what would happen some 450 years later. As Catholics, we pray this psalm on Palm Sunday. "My God, my God, why have you forsaken me? All who see me scoff at me, they mock me."

Mary and Joseph raised Jesus and we know that he was raised in the Jewish faith. He was taught well what it means to be a young Jewish man. When it was time for him to begin his public ministry, we know Joseph had already preceded him in death. And imagine Mary as she watched her son's public ministry.

The last words spoken by Mary in Scripture are the most important for us to hear and they are, "Do whatever he tells you." It was at the wedding feast in Cana where Mary called Jesus to begin his public ministry. She was obedient to God, and Jesus was obedient to her. He turned the water into wine, the first miracle, at the bequest of Mary.

And then of course we know the stories as his ministry unfolded, his teaching, his preaching, and his healing, raising Lazarus from the dead. Mary witnessed them all. We can only imagine the profound impact on her heart and in her life. To see the only son of the widow was raised from the dead and given back to his mother, what a great comfort that would be to Mary. She witnessed the feeding of 5,000 men, plus the women, and children that day. It had to have been a tremendous point of pride for her. But she was always quietly in the background instead of front and center anywhere.

Imagine the impact of hearing her son say, not once, but numerous times, that he would suffer, die, and on the third day be raised. He literally said, "The Son of Man will suffer and die but on the third day I will make all things new." I cannot imagine hearing my son say the words, I am going to die, and not want to jump into the middle of it and say, "Not on my watch, kid." And yet Mary teaches us to be obedient to the will of God, to be obedient and respond to the word of Jesus.

As they drew closer to Jerusalem, knowing that it would be the place he would ultimately suffer and die, her heart must have soared when they entered the city and instead of being greeted with swords and clubs, they were greeted with the entire population crying out, "Hosanna to our king." They laid down their palm branches and their cloaks as he rode astride the donkey and they cried out, "Hosanna! Hosanna! Hosanna!" Even the animal he rode had significance. The donkey rode by King David, King Solomon, and Jesus symbolized peace, not war. Soldiers and warriors rode horses, but prophets and kings rode donkeys as a symbol of peace and work to be accomplished. As he entered Bethlehem, which means *house of bread*, where he was to be born, he was in the womb of Mary astride the donkey and as he entered Jerusalem that prophecy fulfilling day of when he would die, he once again rode a donkey.

Mary must have thought that perhaps things had changed. Perhaps the plan had changed. Look at the way he was being welcomed! Her heart must have been so happy for those brief hours. But we know how sinful is man and how much in need of a Savior we all are. How quickly the crowd changed and in a matter of hours what he foretold was beginning to happen. In the upper room he celebrated Passover, the last supper, the final meal with them, while at the same time instituting the holy Eucharist. Then he went into the garden to pray for strength. Coming out of the Garden of Gethsemane, he was arrested and taken. Mary followed along, staying as close as she could to her son.

What Mary teaches us is that in the dark moments, we stay close to Jesus. We do not run away from him. She watched as Judas betrayed him. She listened as Peter denounced even knowing him. And yet she was faithful. After he had been scourged and beaten, and she saw them push that crown of thorns onto his head, she did not get in the way of the plan. No matter how heart-wrenching it was, she knew that his plan, and not hers, was what was most important.

As they made their way through the city and ultimately to Golgotha, she followed him and loved him. At the end, only she, John, and Mary Magdalene were standing at the foot of the cross. All the others fled. And we learn from her how God takes care of every detail. Knowing that her Joseph had preceded Christ in death and now her only son was about to die, he looked down from the cross and publicly declared, "Woman, behold your son," and to John he said, "Behold your mother." We read in sacred Scripture that from that hour, John took her into his home.

Jesus did not leave anything to chance when it came to Mary. Back in that time, a woman was mere property. It did not matter that she was the mother of the Savior of the world. She was simply property in her time and in that place. Jesus honored her by not leaving her alone. He publicly gave her to John because there were no other children, there was no husband. Mary would have been alone otherwise. In that same statement, "behold your mother," I believe in my heart of hearts that he was also speaking to the rest of us. I can only imagine the memories of his miracles flooded into her mind from her heart giving her the courage and peace she needed to stay through his crucifixion.

Held within Your Heart

Chorus: Who could you go to?
Who could you tell your story to?
Who could ever, ever, ever, ever comprehend,
The life that he'd prepared for you to live?
And there it was in front of you
You heard, you saw, you knew,
And all of this you held within your heart.

You have heard the tidings of the angels.
Their greetings brought the word of God to earth.
Through the voice of Gabriel, God's plan for you revealed
Brought forth your "yes" and then our Savior's birth.
Once the babe was lying in the manger,
The angels spoke to shepherds in the field.
And in dreams of wisemen, too, the message spoke was clear
Gave meaning in your life within your heart concealed. (Chorus)

Angels gave direction for a journey.
They spoke to Joseph once more in a dream
The Christ-child was protected and His life was spared
Until the perfect age of thirty-three.
On Calvary no angel's voice was heard.
The raging crowd was all that filled your ear.
You knew that He could have called ten thousand angels near,
Instead you watched once more in love, in fear....

Bridge: On the morning of the third day following your pain,
You clearly heard the voice of God again.
The tomb was empty, and your Son had risen from the grave.
All your children born in sin from His love now were saved.
(Chorus) And all of this you held within your heart.

We reflect on Mary's unwavering faith in the beautiful image of the *Pieta*. We can learn so much from Mary's disposition when Jesus was taken down from the cross after his death. It really is one of my favorite images to look at and to draw inspiration from when it comes to Mary. To look at her face looking at his face once he had given his life is beyond words.

When I ask people, "What do you see in her expression?" I normally hear responses like sorrow, pain, love, and sometimes the word relief. The word that comes to mind when I ponder her expression is *expectation*. Remember that she heard him say I am going to suffer and die, but on the third day rise. As his mother, you know she was holding onto his words, "But on the third day, I will rise."

Seeing his life through her eyes makes us realize that we need to listen to him and then, as in the words of Mary, do whatever he tells you. When we listen to him, first we realize that there is so much that he will pour into our lives if we will just allow that intimate relationship to be a part of our daily journey. That is what Mary teaches us in her relationship with Jesus, her son. She is looking into his face in that moment and she is saying, "Son, you said on the third day you would rise. I am taking you at your word because everything else that you spoke has come to be."

And we know that he did not disappoint her. We know the beautiful resurrection story! We know the joyful hallelujah shout that went up upon his resurrection and filled Mary with such joy is real.

When I was thinking about these aspects of Mary's life, and the obedience and the love that she calls us to for her son, it was amazing to let those songs resonate during that 33-day period. It seemed like the best title for that entire project would simply be *Lend Me Your Heart*. Because that's what she does. This amazing grace that filled her comes from the Holy Spirit, who offers us the same grace from the moment of our baptism to live with and for him.

One of the phrases that Saint Maximilian Kolbe is known for is, "Don't be afraid to love Mary too much because you will never love her as much as Jesus loves her. She is his mama." When we think of some of the doctrine that surrounds the life of Mary, it just makes sense. One that many Protestant congregations question is Mary's perfection from the moment she was conceived in the womb of Saint Anne. It could not be possible for Jesus Christ to be perfect if he had come from an imperfect mother. Remember the word *conceived* and realize that Mary's DNA is part of Jesus's DNA. She would have had to be perfect from the moment she was conceived in her mother's womb. The rest of us were all conceived in sin and therefore need a Savior. Mary had already been saved before she was conceived. There is another mindblower for you. God knew her heart and he knew that her will would be in perfect accord with his own. Otherwise, she would not have been chosen as the mother of the Savior. Mary used her gift of free will perfectly.

I think one of the most difficult things to overcome with regard to Mary is our own sinfulness. When we see perfection and we want to emulate it, the more perfect it is, the more is required of us to live that way. Mary is both a model for us and a huge stumbling block because we know we are not perfect. The beauty of Mary is she does not expect us to be perfect. She just wants us to love her son. Songs that became part of *Lend Me Your Heart* truly do speak my heart. I want her to help me come closer to her son. She knows him better than any of us ever could.

What is beautiful is that the Holy Spirit that overshadowed her and with whom she conceived Christ is the Holy Spirit that comes upon us when we are baptized and confirmed. It is the same Holy Spirit that fills us with the gifts and the grace that we need from God to live our lives for him. We can take great solace in the fact that the Holy Spirit allows us to use our gift of free will to get to know God, love him, and serve him with our life. What a marvelous realization of the gift of grace.

Thinking about that look on her face in the *Pieta* made me want to have that phrase "I Take You at Your Word" become part of my moment-by-moment living ideal. I do want to take Christ at his word. When he said he gave himself for us, I know he meant it. I opened up John 6:35–66 after thinking about who he says he is in the Eucharist.

Of course, I had to write another recording. This time, I focused completely on Christ as our Eucharistic feast. Be still my heart! First, he asks me to do a record for his mom and then she tells me to never leave it pointed at her, but to take us deeper into his heart and word. So out of obedience I began writing songs about receiving him in the most holy sacrifice of the Mass. I do absolutely take him at his word.

I Take You at Your Word

A maiden fair so long ago was praying in her room.
Your messenger who spoke to her said life was coming soon.
And with her yes, she came to know the Word of God in flesh.
I learned from her to listen well and take you at your word.
The twelve you chose would journey through, three years they'd
spend with you.

You spoke to them in parables, and yet they knew the truth.
Everything you spoke and promised Lord has been fulfilled
So why is it so hard for some to take you at your word?

You spoke so clearly in Capernaum on that day. "Amen, amen,
amen I say to you, unless you take and eat my flesh and take and
drink my blood, you have not life within you.

For those who eat my flesh and drink my blood have lasting life, and I will raise him on the last day." Then how can so many walk away?

Though wheat made bread and grapes pressed down,
there's so much more that's here.
What passed my lips as food Oh Lord, Oh may my heart possess
In purity the love you gave for all eternity
That I may stay this close to you and take you at your word.

My heart is overwhelmed with love, that you would come to me,
In such a way, so intimate, becoming one with me.
No longer bread, no longer wine, but you, my risen Lord.
You gave your life, that I may live, I take you at your word.
I receive you, Precious Lord, I take you at your word.

Chapter 20

Another word that I needed to go deeper into was "manger." It seemed like it just kept popping up. A Scripture passage, song, or picture would pop up and there was the manger. I looked it up.

I could not let go of the word manger or manducate. I realized that the very first place that Jesus Christ allowed himself to be on this earth once he was outside of the living tabernacle of his mother was a manger. That had to mean more than the fact that it was the only clean place in the barn to lay him down. He was inviting us in the Eucharist to literally consume him and gave us a beautiful foreshadowing of this while he was still an infant. The more that I devoured that word, the more it took me to the beautiful Eucharist life that I have the privilege of living as a Catholic.

There are so many places in the world where it is dangerous to go to Mass. You are literally putting your life in danger to go to

Mass. A dear priest friend of mine, Father Jerry, another one of those threads in my tapestry, shared stories of his time in Iraq and Afghanistan serving the military community as a Catholic chaplain. He would have to go in a separate vehicle as the priest from the elements necessary for Mass or he would literally be taking his life into his own hands. He would say Mass, and he would consecrate the bread and the wine into the body and blood of Jesus Christ.

Jesus gave the Great Commission to celebrate the Mass. He instructed the apostles, the first to celebrate the Mass, to take the bread and the wine, and to speak his words of consecration so that we might receive him body and blood, soul and divinity. One of the things that has always been a living proof is that there are some faith communities outside of the Catholic Church that claim to celebrate Jesus Christ as communion. I sincerely pray that I don't offend here, but if you ever notice when Satanic groups try to steal the sacred body of Jesus Christ, it only ever happens from Catholic churches. Satan himself knows when Jesus is truly present in the Eucharist. The reason that they try to take the sacred host is they want to desecrate Jesus Christ. How much more magnificent would it be if every Christian could come back into the church founded by Christ to receive Jesus Christ in the true Eucharist?

I love the hearts of my Protestant friends who love Jesus Christ. I am truly grateful to the men who bring their talents, and it is a privilege to call them brothers in Christ. But I pray that until my last breath, the most important thing that I can do as a recording artist and as an inspirational speaker is to boldly speak the truth in a way that is both inviting and authentic.

Just as I was asked by that record label so many years ago to water it down to make it more palatable, I will never do that because in the words of sacred Scripture the truth will set you free. In order for us to truly use our free will in accordance with God's will, we need to know the truth. It would have been much easier for me many years ago, and probably financially it would have been much more lucrative had I said yes to the label and watered it down. I would not do that back in 1997, I would not do that in 2001, and I'll never do it. To whom much is given, much is expected, and I have been given everything by Jesus Christ.

The Christmas project, *Come to the Manger*, is so much more than singing about baby Jesus simply lying in a manger. It is that realization of who he is, and how he is offering himself to us under the appearance of bread and wine. I want to bring everyone I meet and everyone I know to the fullness of the teachings of the Catholic faith. I want to share the most intimate of embraces, to commune with us in the Eucharist. Again, *manducate* is the Latin word that gives us the invitation and direction of Christ when he said, "Take and eat, this is my body given for you."

Manducate (The Manger)

Manducate, Jesus fill me
Manducate, come receive
Manducate, life eternal
Take and eat the living bread.

In Bethlehem, the house of bread,
was born the lamb of God.
Come and see the newborn King resting in the manger,
in the manger, manducate.

As Mama Mary laid you down
You closed your eyes in slumber.
Not by chance, but you ordained, your body to be laid
in the manger, manducate.
The upper room, the final meal,
Would change everything.
Breaking bread and sharing wine you give us living food.
Manducate, come be fed.

Your holy body lifted up and nailed upon that tree.
Your precious blood poured out to save this world.
Your promise is fulfilled that gave your life indeed
yet remain with us in forms of bread and wine.
Manducate, manducate.

Now, as the soldiers laid you down,
Upon your mother's knee,
We see her tears turn into joy as you kept your word
Resurrected, manducate
From the manger, manducate
In the banquet, manducate

***

It's funny how many times I would hope to hear some feedback on how events in which I participated affected people. Rarely did I hear what I thought I would hear. One in particular that comes to mind was the beautiful Advent mission that I did in Bloomington, Minnesota. It was a lovely event. During that time of year, we prepared for Christ's coming at Christmas. In spite of freezing cold temperatures and lots of snow, the church was full. The children from the religious education department came out and did the most beautiful interpretation of one of my songs. As I sang, they did hand motions and dance and it brought me to tears. It was so beautiful.

A couple of weeks after Christmas, I received an unexpected phone call from a mortician in Minnesota. He asked if I had any family in the Minneapolis–St. Paul area. I told him that I was not aware of any and asked why. He said an elderly woman by the name of Pauline Carrick had passed away. She had no one to come and claim her, no one to make arrangements for her funeral or anything. He was hoping that since we have the same last name that perhaps I was related to her. I told him that I would check with my husband's family since of course Carrick is my married name. After checking with family in Michigan, it was very clear that she was not a relative of ours. I called him back and told him how sorry I was of her passing but that she is not my family.

A few weeks later, he called back. Now I have to admit I had not given her much thought since she was not my family. But when he called back and said no one had yet come forward, it broke my heart to think that this elderly woman died alone. She had been in a Catholic assisted living residence and had no visitors. Other than the staff who were caring for her, she literally died alone. How sad was that? So Kurt and I spoke about it for just a few minutes and I called him back immediately and asked him what we should do. Since we were in Arizona and they were in Minneapolis, I wasn't sure what the expectation would be. He said not to worry, that they could send her to us. That seemed rather strange. Then he explained that she had since been cremated and it would be simple enough to mail or should I say Federal Express her remains to us here in Arizona.

It was the saddest little plastic container inside that FedEx package. Again, it broke my heart to see how a person of her age could be reduced to this little plastic container. Now being in full-time ministry and honestly not knowing what to expect financially again for a funeral, it all felt very awkward and could get expensive quickly. So I went on Craigslist, yes that Craigslist. I found a beautiful pink and cream marble urn. It was $100, and I was thrilled to get it for such a great price. Kurt and I opened up the urn, which was also a vault, and we put her remains into it instead of leaving them in the sad little plastic bag and container.

Next, we had to figure out where her final resting place should be. Again, Minnesota is so far away from Arizona. I called St. John Cantius Church in Free Soil and asked them for the price of a cemetery plot. They said it was a good thing I called them because prices would be going up soon. That day, however, the price was still only $150 for a plot. When Kurt and I heard how amazing the price was, we bought five of them. Keeping in mind that here in Scottsdale, Arizona, a plot could range anywhere from $3,000 to $5,000 and a niche for the urn could be anywhere from $1,500 to $3,000, it was just crazy to hear such a small price. It also made me realize that I would like to be buried in the cemetery of the little tiny parish in Michigan where I had received most of my Sacraments.

What was lovely was Father Kilian came to our home that evening and offered Mass for Pauline. It was funny because he had flown back to the United States after visiting his father in Ireland. Whenever he would go home for a visit, his accent got much more pronounced. After proclaiming the gospel, we all sat down around the dining room table and Father asked the question, "What can we say about dear old Pauline?" I thought, *I've got nothing.*

He went on to say that even though we didn't know her personally, we know when she was born and when she died and all of those years in between were so amazing. All of the advances in technology that she would've witnessed. The Second World War was during her childhood. All of the things that happened in this country and around the world during her lifetime were fascinating. By the time he finished speaking about the time in which she lived, it felt like we had come to know her. I have to admit I actually got a bit teary eyed. How strange, when I had never met this lady.

We agreed that we were not going to simply send her to Free Soil via Federal Express. We would instead take her remains in her beautiful little urn with us when we went on tour that summer. The most beautiful gift of grace was that the sweet little lady who had died alone had an entire family at her gravesite for her internment. You see, my mom and dad were celebrating their 50th wedding anniversary that summer. My entire extended family, my siblings, aunts, uncles, and cousins were all gathering together in the little town of Free Soil. It was so beautiful to have her life truly celebrated.

As she was interred, and we all prayed for her soul to find peace with our Lord, it was beautiful to realize how many people were praying for this woman whom we never met in this life, but I hope to meet in the next. Ever since that day in the cemetery, our family has referred to her as Aunt Pauline.

***

I must share the most recent miracle in my life. Having gone through so many different times where I have seen God's grace come into my life in miraculous ways as well as through healing hands of his physicians, I know it is all grace. It is all a gift. It seems like these experiences were not meant just for me, but to be shared to encourage people to never stop praying. To just embolden the human spirit to look at our Creator and acknowledge he is the source of our strength and our help.

It was only a few days before Thanksgiving 2017 when I went for my annual follow-up oncology appointment. Ever since the lung cancer was removed from me surgically in 2008, I have gone each year for a CT scan of the chest to make sure that we stay ahead of things if ever there would be a recurrence. Well, that year my CT scan came back with a new tumor. This time, it was on the left. It was very small and in fact almost too small for a clean biopsy.

Now, the good news is that over these years since the first time I had lung cancer there are now treatments available, including chemotherapy and specialized radiation, for these types of tumors. And as crazy as it sounds, my oncologist wanted me to wait a few weeks to allow the tumor to grow large enough to get a good biopsy. That would then allow the radiation therapy to begin, after which we would have a better idea about what to look at as far as recurrence rate and ongoing follow-ups.

We had Thanksgiving dinner at our daughter's home, and I can honestly say once again that I'm grateful for cancer. There were a couple of family members who had been estranged and were finding it difficult to reconnect, but when they learned that I had lung cancer there was an immediate healing in the relationship. It's true that life is too short to live in upset or hurt, and we just need to be family. Once again, cancer had healed a division in our family. It was beautiful.

A few days after Thanksgiving, Kurt and I went up to Fort Collins, Colorado, for an Advent mission at the Parish of St. Joseph. At the same time, we were able to visit our son who was on a temporary duty assignment with the air force in Wyoming. His fiancée, Chelsea, came with us so that they could have time together before their upcoming wedding.

While we were all at the Saturday evening vigil Mass, the priest who was praying the Mass offered the Sacrament of the anointing of the sick for anyone who would like to receive that directly after Mass. Needless to say, I was excited to be able to receive the anointing. With the recurrent diagnosis just a few days prior, I had not been able to receive that gift yet. So after Mass I lined up with a number of other people who were there. It felt so good to feel that peacefulness and strength surrounding me.

One of the lovely gifts that evening was that the deacon assisting Father was holding a first-class relic of Saint Peregrine. He is the patron saint for those suffering from cancer. When it was my turn to step forward, I held that relic in my hand for just a few minutes while the person in front of me received the anointing Sacrament. I handed the reliquary back to the deacon, stepped forward, and put my hands out as Father gave me the beautiful gift of the Sacrament.

As he made the sign of the cross on my forehead and as he blessed my hands with the oil of anointing, I felt a heat go through my chest cavity like I've never felt before in my life. The intense warmth was powerful and tender in the same moment. Then I felt tears flow out of my eyes, not tears of any kind of sadness, but just an overwhelming presence of God. It was like it was too much for me to hold and it came out as tears.

After I spent a few minutes in the church just thanking God for his gift of peace in the midst of this cancer, I went out into the vestibule where Kurt, Paul, and Chelsea were taking care of our table with CDs and other things that we have at our events. When I walked up to the table, I could feel this big smile on my face, and I told Kurt that I would not be surprised if that when they went to start my radiation treatments that they wouldn't be able to find the tumor.

When the day came for me to begin the radiation treatments, the first step of course is to do a CT scan, set the markers for where the radiation will be given, and then start the therapy. The oncologist radiologist ran the CT scan in his office, and then I was asked to go into the exam room and wait for him. I went into the exam room and Kurt was there with me.

The oncologist radiologist came in, turned on the screen, and pointed at the tumor that they had found in November. Then he went to the current screen and pointed at the same spot in my lung. While scratching his head he said, "We can't find it." It was crazy! I was so excited. And it was so funny that the physician kept saying almost apologetically that they could not find my tumor.

I did not have to have radiation; I did not have to have chemotherapy. God had decided to literally allow this one to be a miracle of supernatural healing. Can I tell you how delighted I was to just be healed? With our son's wedding happening in that time frame, I was ecstatic there was not one second of focus on me, but only on him and his bride as they prepared for their Sacrament and the celebration of our growing family.

This incredible unfailing grace that God offers us can be so easily overlooked until we can see him in every single detail of our lives. Many times, it would be easy to use the word coincidence or life incidents when, in fact, God is literally in every one of the details.

Chapter 21

M y aunt Lenida is an incredible woman of faith. When she went into hospice, it was so beautiful to see the way that she embraced death knowing that she would be going home to her Lord. Much like her sister, my aunt Patricia, my godmother, did.

I had the privilege of taking my mom, who had just turned 80, back to Michigan to be with her sister while she was dying. It was December, so of course in Michigan that meant very cold weather. My cousin Dan came into my aunt's room and showed me a picture on his cell phone. It was the most beautiful design I have ever seen in glass. He said that one of his employees at work asked him how much that design work had set him back financially. He chuckled and said not one dime.

As I looked closer at the glass in the picture, I realized it was frost. With that image in mind, I spent the next day and a half at my aunt's bedside along with her children and my mom and watched in absolute awe the love that was shared in the room. Here was a woman in her late 80s who had spent her entire life loving God, loving her family, and asking for the intercession of sweet Mama Mary. Now it was her time to go home. There was no upset, there was no anger that death would soon take her, there was only the most amazing love that filled every part of that building. Every one of us was able to tell her that we loved her and to thank her for being the witness that she had been throughout our lives.

The sweet lady, who had baked more pies, made more cakes, and served more casseroles for potlucks over the years than could be counted, was getting ready to go home to her reward. After she had exhaled for the last time and we sat together in the room knowing that her spirit was going home to the Lord, there was a sense of relief that her pain was finished. I also had this simple knowing that her final breath was the last gift on this side of heaven.

Remembering that every breath we breathe is a gift from God, seeing the beauty in creation and something so simple as frost opened my eyes, my heart, and my emotion to the simple and magnificent fact that God is literally in every single detail. I had no intention of writing a song that day, but once her body had been taken to the mortuary to be prepared for her funeral, and my cousins had all gone home for some much needed rest, I sat down and allowed the Holy Spirit to move me.

Realizing that in just a few weeks it would be Christmas, I saw all of the houses that were already being decorated for the festivities of the season and the beauty in the frost. I realized that creation herself was preparing to receive the newborn King.

In the Book of Daniel the prophet, we read that everything on this earth gives honor and glory to God. We, the creatures of our Creator, should be offering that kind of praise in every moment of every day of our life. When frost and chill, snow and rain, beasts wild and tame can give honor and glory to God by virtue of being created by him, how much more can we give him praise, adoration, and love? Sometimes it's in the simple details that God is revealed in the most magnificent way.

Creation Receive Your King

Crystal flakes of falling snow, frosted paintings on the windows
No human hand could render such perfection.
Such majestic water frozen by the Master's Touch,
creation is preparing to receive her king.

Let the earth bless the Lord; Praise him over all forever.
and every living being worship the Creator.

Sun and moon, bless the Lord; Stars of heaven, bless the Lord.
Nights and days, bless the Lord. Light and darkness,
bless the Lord;

Hallelujah. Hallelujah. Hallelujah O Creation receive your King.

Fire and heat, bless the Lord; Cold and chill, bless the Lord.
Dew and rain, bless the Lord; Ice and snow, bless the Lord;

Hallelujah. Hallelujah. Hallelujah O Creation receive your King.

Wild and tame, bless the Lord; Life and breath, bless the Lord;
Man and woman, bless the Lord; Every heartbeat, bless the Lord;

Hallelujah. Hallelujah. Hallelujah O Creation receive your King.
In each perfect snowflake the Father's joy is present.
Still more, lovely than creation, is the infant.
From the womb of Holy Mary, comes the newborn King.
The love of God for all declared in this union.

Let the earth bless the Lord; Praise him over all forever.
and every living being worship the Creator.

Hallelujah. Hallelujah. Hallelujah O Creation receive your King.

***

Over the weeks and months that I've taken to write this book, I have been overwhelmed by the generosity of God's love in my life. On one particular writing day, I was in a hotel in West Monroe, Louisiana, and I found myself after a few hours of writing, kneeling down on the floor next to the bed in the hotel room and allowing the tears to flow.

What a magnificent God who loves us. What an incredible holy mother Mary who is willing to journey with us. I know myself. I know that I am not worthy of any of these blessings, and yet that's the beauty of unfailing grace. It is gift. None of us is ever worthy, but that doesn't stop God from pouring his grace into our lives.

Chapter 22

With grace, what does real forgiveness look like? It has different faces depending on the situation we experience in our lives. When I think about the strength of my daughter Edel and the way her son came into the world, it was more simple to forgive the people responsible for her rape. Honestly, it wasn't until I heard her words of forgiveness towards the man and the rest of those involved the day of the attack that I was even open to true forgiveness. As a family we received the gift of an infant, her precious child whose very life brought some sense of purpose out of her suffering. The images in my mind of someone hurting my daughter in such a horrible way have never gone away. When I watch a television show, a movie, or even the news and I hear the word rape, or see a violent action, I feel myself tense up just a little and my heart goes out to my daughter. But somehow over these years, the intensity of the emotion has dimmed along with the grace of being able to forgive from my heart. I honestly don't know how I would react should I ever meet those involved face-to-face, but I only hope that the gift of Zachary's life and Edel's healing would outweigh any malice from me.

Recently, however, I was given the challenge of coming face-to-face with my own heart and soul over a deep pain that my family experienced over 20 years ago. One of my brothers was concerned about his step-grandchildren who lived in another state. He and his wife went for an unannounced visit and found the household in a very dangerous situation. The extreme use of drugs by the parents of the children and the filthy condition of the home made them want to step in and make sure the children were removed for safety's sake. They contacted the authorities and told them they would like to have temporary custody of the four little ones until such time as their daughter and her boyfriend could get clean and properly care for their children.

Instead of allowing any of the extended family to take the children into our good, clean, safe homes the authorities took control and put the children into foster care. It was so strange to find out that my nieces and nephews were put into a home with a family who did not speak English. These children did not speak Spanish as the foster family did. We were able to visit them once during the time they were with the foster family but only at the state child welfare facility. While we were visiting with the children, my four-year-old nephew Kristian was being protective of the three younger siblings. When we would reach out to pick up or hug one of the kiddos, he would stand in between us and them and directly watch us. Then after a couple of minutes, he would allow us to proceed with our playtime. After our visit, the social workers came in to get the four children ready to take back to the foster home. I told them about Kristian's behavior and they brushed it off. We went back to Arizona and continued praying for the family. Our son, Paul, and Kristian were only three months apart in age. They were so cute together when they would play during visits. Knowing that the little cousins were in such turmoil made me so sad for them. It was only a couple of weeks later that my brother called and told us that little Kristian had been killed! We were shocked! Maria, the foster care woman, had literally beaten this little four-year-old boy to death.

It was like we had become part of a crazy nightmare as we listened to police reports and saw the story of this little one's death on the evening news. The agony that I heard in my sister-in-law's and brother's voices was so painful. They had only wanted to help their sweet grandchildren and now one of them had been killed and the other three had been seriously damaged physically and emotionally by the traumas they had endured. They told us when the funeral would be, and we all met to honor Kristian's life and weep together at this sad loss. Then the criminal investigations began. The court dates proceeded one after another until finally the hearings were done and Maria was found guilty of three counts of child abuse, three counts of child endangerment, and one count of murder. She was sentenced to prison for 15 years to life.

We each mourned Kristian's death in our own way. I watched as my brother and sister-in-law moved forward day by day in their lives. Even though we all move forward, we never forget our loved ones. The pain of loss over the years began to ease. Fifteen years had gone by before we knew it. Over those years, every person related to Kristian had continued to live their life. One of his sisters had been pretty seriously hurt by Maria, and to this day lives in a special needs community near to her brother and father. One of his sisters stayed closer to their mother, who eventually moved to another state. His cousins all grew up and have lived their lives. It wasn't until those 15 years had passed that we had even really given any thought to what Maria's life might be like in prison. The reason we began to think about Maria after all these years was that she was now eligible to begin the process for parole hearings.

When the first one was sought, we were contacted by the District Attorney's office and told about our rights as family of the victim. It was insane to have to sit there and listen to every single gruesome detail of Kristian's death. What his little body looked like, the coroner's report, and on and on. I felt sick as I listened. Finally, it was time for family members to each give a statement. My brother could not be there physically but had sent a letter that was read in the court. My sister-in-law had passed away from a heart attack four years prior. My mother and father had written a letter as well and it was read. I was attending via telephone, so I was able to tell her what I thought of her and how many of the family gatherings and milestones Kristian had missed because of her. Maria continued to make excuses for her actions, blaming her anger that fateful day on four defenseless children who were in her care. I was not ready to forgive her. Over the next seven years, there would be a total of three more of these parole hearings. Each one as painful as the first. Each one I would pray beforehand because I would begin to feel the anxiety of the pending hearing date and I would try to prepare myself for the horrific reliving of the events that ended the life of this tiny little child who had been so full of life. During each hearing, I would hear Maria's voice as she spoke and then hear it repeated as she had her translator speak for her in English. Each year, I would imagine what his life could have been if he had not been so brutally killed. Knowing that he and Paul were the same age, I reflected on the fact that I had watched my son graduate from high school, begin college, join the air force, and get married. I couldn't help but wonder what Kristian would have experienced in this same time.

In all these years, I had not allowed forgiveness to be a part of my thoughts as I would participate in the parole hearings. Then it happened. The next hearing was beginning. The phone lines connected and I waited to be introduced into the proceedings. I prayed to God that his justice would happen again. I did not want this monster freed from prison to cause more pain and suffering to anyone else. This time, there was a different feeling in the courtroom. We were told ahead of time that we would not have to listen to the details of the murder again. They said we would be focusing on what Maria had been doing for the last two years to be rehabilitated. But in the course of three hours, I heard voices again in the courtroom give a number of details about what had happened over 20 years prior. This time, though, Maria began to weep. She begged for pardon. She told the family who was there in the courtroom and by phone that she was so sorry for killing Kristian. For the first time, she admitted to what she had done and when asked for the details by the attorneys and commissioner, she cried as she gave the savage description of how he died that day at her hand. Then I heard Kristian's father's voice. He said that as Christians we are called to forgive but he wasn't sure if he could yet. He went on to admit that the way he was living back in the day was why his children were taken from him and placed in harm's way. He owned that. But he also spoke about honoring his son's life after it was so brutally taken. He had gone to college to earn a bachelor's degree in psychology and a master's degree in social work. He was spending his life caring for others in honor of his son. He admitted that 23 years was a long time for her to be in prison, but that 23 years was not a long time to have a child. He should still be with us. He admitted that he was trying to forgive.

I wept for him and then I was surprised as I found myself crying for Maria. She spoke about her husband, who has remained married to her for these 23 years. She spoke about her two adult children, who are now married and have children of their own. She admitted that she had been a monster and treated the four little ones worse than animals. She said she was so sorry. When it was my turn to speak, I told her that I appreciated her finally telling the truth and her contrite heart. I told her that since this was so new that perhaps she needed some time to remain incarcerated until she could figure out what that means. Once I finished my speech, I felt kind of numb. I also felt like I had been sitting in judgment of someone. I knew I needed to actually hear her and forgive her, but I was not ready yet. I just wasn't ready to hear that she should be free. There was a short recess as the deliberation happened. Twenty minutes seemed like an eternity and then the commissioner began to speak. He said, "After all the material today has been reviewed, it is my decision that Maria is suitable for parole." As much as I was still confused with my own thoughts and feelings, I could hear grace trying to climb into my heart. I could feel the heaviness of evil trying to fight against the love that was attempting to soften my emotions and allow forgiveness to enter. So many times, I have literally told people in the events that I do around the country that they need to realize that no soul should ever be lost. Every time we refuse to forgive and think that darkness has won, we are admitting that the beautiful prize of someone's soul has been taken by Satan. No soul should ever be lost to Satan. We all belong to God. And here I was refusing to forgive. Once the hearing was over, I went into the chapel in Sacred Heart Church and sat in front of the tabernacle. I needed to be close to Jesus and ask him to help me. What a crazy day it had been! I was in the middle of a national ministry tour going from parish to parish across the country on our tour bus. I had actually been sitting in the coach, in the church parking lot, wired into this telephonic parole hearing.

The same day, another extended family member needed safe shelter, having just been released from the hospital after being beaten to within an inch of her life from the man she trusted. On one hand, I was supposed to be forgiving someone who had killed a child 23 years prior and at the same time help another family member who was in such pain. God, where is this unfailing grace that I talk about? As soon as I asked, it flooded through me once again. God's grace filled me. I was indeed able to see Maria as a child of God. She needed healing as much as any of us does. She needs grace in her life to be able to go forward and resume life outside of prison at 61 years old. The way grace will continue to be able to work in me is when I will let it in not only when I want it, but when God knows I need it. She will be in my daily prayers for peace, strength, and healing and so that no soul may be lost. And so begins the next journey of needing and utilizing grace as I help another person from my extended family. We are allowed righteous anger when someone is being hurt, and we stand in the gap when we must. We cannot, however, judge someone. That is only for God to do. To make sense of it and find peace in the journey is only possible by the real presence of God in our daily life.

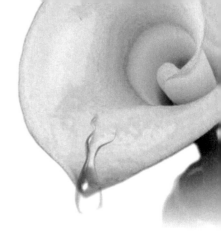

Chapter 23

Life can be messy. Life can be full of pain, suffering, sorrows, and times we feel like we want to just give up. But if we can begin to look at every breath as a gift, if we can begin to see each person who God introduces into our life as another soul filled with his grace, when we began to embrace the daily blessings and never take them for granted, we will be able to realize that we are living truly in unfailing grace. Grace is there in the incredible joy of marriage, the incredible gift of new life in our children and our grandchildren. I see in concrete ways that God is present in each and every member of my family; this is a gift. This is grace.

As I have watched my adult children get married and begin their families, I see that they will have their joys and their sorrows, their trials and their triumphs. I know that God, through his Holy Spirit, that same beautiful Holy Spirit who touched my life at such a young age, fills each one of these beautiful people exactly the same way as he filled me.

He fills each and every one of us the same way. In baptism, our soul is introduced to God and then throughout our life he fills us with exactly what we need so that someday when we close our eyes in death, our soul will journey home to our Maker, our Creator, our King and Savior. How beautiful that he allows his own mother, Mama Mary, to stand in the gap for us and with us. I love that she is part of his unfailing grace.

An important thought for this book is a little prayer. It ultimately became a song that I would sing for my children and grandchildren. It's called "From Mother to Mother" and in a simple way just speaks my heart that there are days when it's hard, those days when we can wander off course, there are days when we push the grace away, but she is constantly standing in the gap and she's constantly taking us, her children, closer to the heart of her son.

I don't mind flat kneecaps if it means that prayers prayed from the heart make a difference and aid in grace. As my Heidi came in one day when I was praying through this song, she encouraged me to share it. She said I was not the only one with flat kneecaps praying for those I love. I am glad I listened to my daughter. She, too, is a mother praying for her littles, Dominic, Madison, and Aaron. She has helped me to share more of my personal stories simply by allowing life in this family to be lived boldly, no matter what.

From Mother to Mother

Mother Mary full of grace would you help me please,
Guide my daughter to the heart of Jesus?
Evil in the world is coaxing her away.
Sins of flesh, of soul, of heart enticing
Darkness of sin tugs at her soul and she needs grace.

From mother to mother,
I know you know my heart is true.
From mother to mother,
I place my girls with you.
Knowing you will take them to your Son,
Helping me until this work is done.
Interceding for us 'til battle's won.

Mama Mary, filled with love, please direct my son,
Take him deep into the heart of Jesus.
Evil in the world is tempting him today.
Sins of flesh, of soul, of heart enticing.
Darkness of sin tugs at his soul and he needs grace.

From mother to mother,
I know you know my heart is true.
From mother to mother,
I place my son with you.
Knowing you will take him to your Son,
Helping me until this work is done.
Interceding for us 'til battle's won.

.

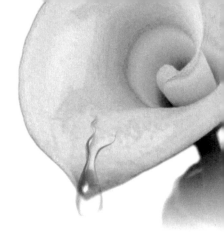

Chapter 24

When I think back to the two little boys, Timmy and Clancy, that we miscarried so many years ago, this book would not be complete if I didn't share the song that I wrote for them. What started as simply a post on Facebook to encourage people to respect life in the womb turned into something much more beautiful and much more healing than I ever expected. It was another proof of unfailing grace. My hope was to share a story about the tender life of each of these babies and in doing so to help people simply cherish life in the womb.

For some reason, for over 30 years I could not bring myself to finish their song. But when I acknowledged their place in the communion of saints, that they are literally standing next to our Lord Jesus Christ, our father God in heaven, the words just simply appeared on paper that day. They are not angels, as so many people refer to babies who are lost to miscarriage. They are saints.

The Christian belief is that when a person is baptized, they enter their life with Christ. When a person dies before the age of reason, before any time that they would be culpable for sin, that soul is perfect and goes home to the Lord. When a child dies from the womb, we know that if they had been born in the normal timeline and would have been baptized, the baptism of desire covers that soul, which means that a child who dies from the womb to miscarriage becomes a saint. And children who die in the womb from elective abortion are martyrs.

These incredible little saints are fully grown in the kingdom of heaven. They intercede for us. They are with us every second of every day, praying for us. If we believe that those who grow up in this world and go home to the Lord are praying for us, then how could we question that those we have carried in our womb would not be doing the same thing?

My husband and I designed this necklace and coin in honor of
our St. Timmy, St. Clancy, and all Baby Saints.

For more information, please visit www.JulieCarrick.com.

Little Saint of Mine (For Timmy & Clancy)

For years, I've tried to share the story of your life,
To put my pen to page to show my heart.
Your precious life, my child, ended far too soon,
As you went to heaven from within my womb.
From the second you were first conceived,
the journey of a saint had just begun.
Unlike the rest of us who run the race for years,
Jesus knew your soul was ready to come home.

Refrain: Little one, child of mine, but first you are a child of God.
He chose me as your mom, to love and carry you,
though I know you first belong to Him.
Now live in peace until we meet again. Oh,
live in peace until we meet again.

Your name is spoken daily as I kneel to pray.
You hear me in communion with the saints.
It seems a little strange to ask a babe to pray,
Oh, but pray for us little saint of mine.
Oh, pray for us little saint of mine.

Bridge: Your heart beneath my heart with a rhythm all your own,
strong and steady leading to the day when I would hold you in my
arms and kiss your tiny face, my little one.
A life spent loving God a hundred years or just for days,
You're in His embrace, we both sing His praise. (Refrain)

Someday, my mind will teach my broken heart to mend.
I'll accept that God knew I could be this strong.
And on that day of grace, when we meet face-to-face,
I will thank the Lord that I could be your mom.
Oh, I thank God that I could be your mom. (Refrain)

After I had shared the song through Facebook Live, it was splendid to see over 4,000 people either share the names of their saints or finally name their children. It made me think of the funny comment our son, Paul, had said back many years ago when we told him along with his sisters that their sibling saints are in heaven praying for us. Paul said, "It's a good thing that you named the boys because otherwise when you get to heaven they could meet you at the gate and say, 'Geez, Mom, there's a guy here named Chrysogonus, and you couldn't come up with a name for us!'" One other time, we were having dinner and the girls were already in their teens while Paul was about six years old. The conversation was one of those loud ones where there was some disagreement about what they should be able to do because their friends were all doing it. Paul simply stated, "I think I know why God had Timmy and Clancy come home early." I asked him why. He continued, "He knew you were going to need some extra saints in heaven to help you with these girls." Once the laughter stopped, I had to admit he might have a valid point about the intercession of our children saints in our life.

It was beautiful to know that our daughters grew up knowing that they have sibling saints in heaven, and then of course after Paul was born and safely raised in our family for him to know that his brother saints prayed along with us every day. It gives such a personal credence in the communion of saints. Someday when we close our eyes in death and we are reunited with our Creator, our God and Savior in heaven, how lovely that we will also see these beautiful saints of ours.

My hope is that every man and woman who conceive a child will acknowledge the beauty of that life. It would be so simple to acknowledge the gift of life and never have to question whether or not the child could be aborted through elective abortion. The healing that has come for those who have succumbed to the acceptance of elective abortion and later regretted it have also shared with me how healing the song, "Little Saint of Mine," is for them.

I do not take one of the songs that I have written for granted. I know that God has his word and voice in the melody and lyric over these years of writing and composing. They all come from him.

***

These are some of the stories of grace in my life. I know you have stories that, if not the same, are similar. Even though I was allowed to suffer trials and sadness in my life, I know beyond any shadow of a doubt that God was with me in every single moment. Fully aware that my marriage could have ended in divorce, I know it was God's grace that allowed not only healing but true joy to be made anew.

Our daughter Edel played the hand dealt to her and came out the other side inspiring so many people to choose life and to avoid the pain of elective abortion. Mama Mary quietly but firmly holds our hands as she shows us how to trust in the darkest moments of despair even when we think we have given in to God's plan. She absolutely knows what it feels like to hand her life over in trust and yet go through extreme life events while loving God in every moment. Learning to find and acknowledge the everyday moments of life and see the deeper and lasting gift of grace is beyond joy—it is finding peace amid everything going on around us.

As of today, Kurt and I continue to travel the country offering events of all sizes and have added a number of artists to our Carrick Ministries Foundation family. Edel is married to Adam, a great guy who adopted Zachary, and gave us the bonus of two more grandsons, Kai and Zuri. Paul and Chelsea are married and living life as an air force family. Heidi is engaged to Wayne, a wonderful man, and we will be planning a wedding soon. Grandchildren are the best!

My sister Lori got to meet her beautiful daughter in September 2018. What grace as these incredible women are getting to know each other. I have also been able to share some of the stories with her daughter, the impact her life has made in many ways. "Kateri" was so much more than a song. I think she knows she is loved to the moon and back.

Prayer is the key. As I wake up each day, even before I open my eyes, I simply say, "This is the day the Lord has made. Let us rejoice and be glad." Kurt sometimes says it before I do and then I get to answer. Then whether we begin with Mass, having some time in the adoration chapel, praying the divine office, or simply having a cup of coffee and chatting with God about our hopes and dreams for that moment in the kitchen, the day is blessed because He is invited and welcomed to journey with us.

I pray his unfailing grace is revealed over and over in your life just as it has been revealed in mine.

Resources and Wonderful Reading to Consider

QR Code and Website Link to learn more about Carrick Ministries Non-Profit Foundation, Artists and Speakers: www.CarrickMinistries.com {501 C-3}

Some of My Favorite Books

Eucharist by Bishop Robert Barron
The Eucharist by Fr. Mitch Pacwa
Manual For Men by Bishop Thomas Olmsted
Consoling the Heart of Jesus by Fr. Michael Gaitley
33 Days to Morning Glory by Fr. Michael Gaitley
Mary-Virgin, Mother, and Queen by Fr. Mitch Pacwa
Surprised By Truth (Vol. 1, 2, 3) by Patrick Madrid
My Daily Bread by Anthony J. Paone S.J.
Catechism of the Catholic Church
Compendium: Catechism of the Catholic Church

Holy Bible (These editions are my favorites because they have all the original books within and are both accurate and beautiful in their translations.)

> New Jerusalem Bible
> Revised Standard Version, Catholic Edition
> New American Bible, St. Joseph Edition
> The Living Bible, Catholic Edition

The Rule of Saint Benedict by Saint Benedict

(*The Rule of Saint Benedict* can apply to anyone in any community setting, whether in the monastery or in your family! Written in the sixth century by the father of monasticism, Saint Benedict himself, this is a common-sense guide to living a truly Christian life. Learn from the Rule's wonderful discretion, moderation, and keen insight into the capabilities and weaknesses of human nature. Here is a practical approach to arranging life so that Christian spirituality and virtue can be lived out anytime, anywhere.)

If you are interested in learning more about the teachings of the Catholic faith or if reading *Unfailing Grace* has sparked your desire to join or return to the Catholic faith, a great way to go deeper is to contact a local Catholic Church near you and join the R.C.I.A. (Rite of Christian Initiation of Adults) or R.C.I.C. (Rite of Christian Initiation of Children) study group. Attending the classes does not require you to become Catholic, but if you so desire to, in the process, then you will joyfully be brought into full communion. Most commonly Holy Saturday, or the evening before Easter Sunday, is when most who have completed the study are welcomed into the faith. Here is a link to Catholic churches in every city: www.MassTimes.org.

Julie Carrick Music Albums

"Come to The Manger" The beauty of Christmas like you have never experienced before. The most lovely ballads of the promise of our Salvation being fulfilled and offered to us from the manger. 14 songs that will inspire you not just for Christmas, but for every single day of the year.

"Hymns of Praise" Traditional Hymns sung by Julie at the request of so many across the country. Plus, Julie's newest song *"Little Saint of Mine"* and a favorite contemporary hymn that reminds us to never stop singing the praise of God. This is a must for every music library.

"I Take You At Your Word" 15 inspired songs about our Precious Lord Jesus Christ in the Holy Eucharist. New songs as well as timeless favorites. This record will invite you to accept the incredible intimacy that Jesus offers each of us in the most Holy Sacrament of the Altar.

"Lend Me Your Heart" 16 Songs honoring the Woman chosen by God. 9 NEW Marian Songs! Inspired by Fr. Michael Gaitley's book *33 Days to Morning Glory*, this album is full of the most beautiful moments that take you through a mother's heart and deep into the heart of her Son.

"In The Waiting" For all who have been touched by cancer. This CD is filled with music to encourage, inspire, and honor all those who are concerned by cancer or other large life events. It is a healing salve to anxious hearts.

"Shades of Grace" Songs each with a specific focus on how we receive God's grace. Sacraments, Daily Life, Prayer. As you listen to these songs, you will sip on the empowering grace of the God who simply loves you. Kurt joins Julie in this grace-focused album.

"The Face of God Collection" This album was beautifully remastered with new songs! It invites us to find the Face of God in His beautiful Eucharistic presence, and in those we are allowed to meet and journey with in this world. 16 amazing songs!

"The Bridge ~ Compilation" This album invites us to acknowledge our sin, but realize the power of Forgiveness and the Mercy of Jesus. Inspired from the Jubilee year Holy Lands concert tour. This record has 16 awe-inspiring songs.

Acknowledgements

I wish to say thank you to so many folks who were instrumental in the book coming to life. As I began the year, I had no idea this labor of love would be such a major part of it. I always thought my husband would write a book since writing comes so natural to him. Now he has no more excuses. In all sincerity, I do thank my husband so very much for allowing me to share more of our story than ever before. In our national ministry of music and spoken word, we had revealed quite a bit in order for people attending our parish missions and conferences to know that what we share is real. We are not just giving abstract ideas but real-life experiences that are able to be lived fully by God's grace. As you listened to the songs, I hope you heard my heart as much as my voice in the music and lyric.

I am so grateful to my sweet *chadults*, Edel, Heidi, and Paul, for allowing me to share so much of their story. When you are family and one of your members is a nationally known recording artist and speaker, there is really not much anonymity. There certainly can be, but when all the members allow the full story to be shared it makes for a much fuller experience for the folks who come to the events. People know when they are getting only part of the story, and it makes it harder for them to truly trust. My beautiful family has allowed such grace to be shared by simply being themselves and trusting me to good stewardship of our family story. Both Edel and Heidi have also shared their gift of music over the years, and all I can say is WOW. When you see their names listed as Guest Vocalist on a recording, you are in for a musical treat. Also, most of the photography captured and artwork designed in the years between 2005 and 2015 were the beautiful work and gift of Paul. They are truly a family that keeps on giving.

The 30th day of Lent was a pivotal day for this book. I had been on a regional Lenten parish mission tour, and every single day I was asked when I would write my book. Each time, I explained that I didn't see myself as an author and carried on. On day 30 as I prayed morning prayer, I asked the Lord to please speak clearly to me that if I was supposed to write a book he would ask me to do so through someone of authority in my life. Two hours later, I was having breakfast with Kurt, and with Janice and Rhett, two of the board members of our non-profit foundation. Halfway through the meal Janice simply stated, "You should write a book." That in and of itself was perfectly timed for me to want to laugh at the audacity of the Holy Spirit, but when Rhett, who is always the voice of reason, chimed in and agreed that it had to be done, I knew I would be busy writing. I am so grateful to this beautiful couple, who has shared so many of the joys and sorrows in our life and ministry. My tapestry would not be complete without them.

They, of course, introduced me to the team at Paper Raven Books. Morgan Gist MacDonald, Karen Furr, Jennifer Crosswhite, Brian Dooley, Jesus Cordero, Shena Sabens, Joe Walters, Claudia Sanchez, Joy Xiang, Amanda Kuebler, Victoria Klein, and Rachela Brisindi are the most amazing, talented, and giving team. I have to say that when I had previously looked at the possibility of a book coming out of someone at Carrick Ministries, I had researched many publishers. It was a sad fact that it was not much different than the record labels who claim to have the artists' best interests at heart only to find out the artist would spend their talents making money for the label. With the Paper Raven Team, it is completely different. The authors literally own their book in its entirety. They help with every step of the process from the initial manuscript review, the editing processes, layout, design, getting it ready and loaded for online as well as paperback and hardcover printing. They are honest while being supportive and keep you on task in a way that is amazing. I am so grateful for each and every one of these talented folks. When I record a new music project, all the session musicians are listed; the studio engineers and all who work on the project are listed. I am so grateful to be able to say THANK YOU to all of these amazing people on my team. I know that God is blessing each and every one of you for all your good work.

Speaking of a team who brings beauty and completion to my work and writings, I just have to acknowledge the musicians whom you are hearing in the music in this book. Gary Lunn, Dave Cleveland, Steven Brewster, Jason Webb, Blair Masters, Mark Hill, Pat McGrath, David Davidson, Roland Mains, Richard Palalay, Randy Melson, Dane Clark, Mark Pay, Steve Dady, Sam Levine, Scott Leader, Zack Clark, Heidi Carrick, and all the beautiful background vocalists who complete the beauty of voice in the recordings. When I think that someday we shall all be with our precious Lord in heaven, oh the sheer magnificence of song praising God we are going to experience for eternity!

Thanks for the sneak peek experience here on earth as you share your talents within the music I have written.

Thank you, Adam Stein, for the lovely headshot. Over the years, I have shied away from my photo being on my recorded music projects. I believe the image on the cover should be about the content within, and since my music is about the Lord and what He is doing, that has become so simple. You captured my expression perfectly for this book.

I am grateful to my mom and daddy, Ted and Joan. They brought me up in the Catholic faith and from the time I was an infant they made sure I knew Christ Jesus. Watching them go through 60 years of marriage with all the joys and sorrows and stories that are their life, as they lived only by God's grace, was such encouragement. Remember, I was one of the seven children they birthed and raised. They, too, have saints in heaven, four to be exact. Imagine how immense their story would be in print!

I am thankful for my extended family and for each and every one of you who has witnessed God's love to me and kept me on the straight and narrow. You know who you are and I love you.

Finally, I am indebted for every single opportunity that God has allowed in my life to meet so many people from every possible walk and situation who have shared their story with me. To know that in a small way my life has made a difference in their journey is such grace. To see how Mama Mary loves them and Christ Jesus holds them gives me the strength to stay in ministry.

Cyndy Carstens, artist and friend, thank for the beautiful logo that you designed and drew for me. It, like you, is lovely.

Thank you for buying and reading this book and for allowing me to share my journey with you. May God bless you and keep you.

About the Author

Internationally known for her music and speaking engagements, Julie Carrick is a Catholic, wife, mother, and friend from Scottsdale, Arizona. One of the most effective speakers and artists in the Catholic Church today, she brings a passionate message of faith, hope, and love masterfully woven through her music and personal witness to living the faith. A veteran singer and composer, she has been featured at countless local, diocesan, national, and international events. As a radio host heard on stations across the U.S., she boldly shares her faith. Her voice is angelic and her lyric truly shares a bounty of grace and wisdom. She is the founder of Catechetical Artistry and co-founder of the Carrick Ministries Foundation and has 20+ years of ministry experience. With 15 awe-inspiring recordings, she shares the emotional element that takes the message of God's love from the head to the heart.

Julie has spent her life going deep into the teachings of the faith, to experience a deep love relationship with Christ inside the church he established over two millennia ago. Her life's work and joy has been to be a Christian wife to her husband, Kurt, to be a mother to her children and bring them up in the faith and then to share that faith through her ministry of music and spoken word. Born and raised in Michigan and then living in Arizona, Germany, and Pennsylvania she has continued a life-long study of sacred scripture. In her itinerant ministry, she has traveled the globe bringing a witness of how to live it in daily life. Desiring to better live the Word of God in her own life, she has looked to the lives of the saints to figure out how they were able to do it. With a deep devotion to the greatest saint of all, Mary, the mother of Christ, she has sought out what it means to allow grace to be her strength. Even with such a lovely title as Christian Recording Artist, her life has been anything but easy. It has, however, been filled with grace beyond measure. After reading Julie Carrick's stories of grace, hopefully you have recognized how much God wants you here, even when it doesn't feel like it. These stories will keep you going on your path when life is at its most difficult, and they will inspire you to discover the grace in your life and how faith can give you the strength to carry on. They will also be your source of joy.

Julie resides in Scottsdale, Arizona and when she is not somewhere on this planet sharing the message of grace at a conference or parish, she is spending time with her family and close friends. She is a parishioner at Blessed Sacrament Parish. She thoroughly enjoys her kitchen and making delicious meals for gatherings in her home. Nona days with her grandchildren are sacred and filled with tea parties, playing cards and board games. She loves to be at her beautiful baby grand piano in her living room, allowing the musings that happen during Eucharistic Adoration to become finished songs. She and Kurt find such peaceful time together just being in and caring for their home together. And whenever possible, she still loves to go horseback riding.

Awards Received by Julie

2006 - United Catholic Music & Video Association's Spoken Word Recording of the Year

2004 - United Catholic Music & Video Association's Artist of the Year

2003 - Nine Awards for her participation in the 9/11 Project "You Are Not Alone"

1997 - The Academy of Independent Recording Artists awarded Julie the Honors of: Single of the Year & Female Vocalist of the Year

1987 - 3rd Infantry Division Wuerzburg Germany Awarded Julie the Army Meritorious Service Award

1985 - 123rd Signal Battalion Wuerzburg, Germany awarded Julie the Outstanding Civilian Service Award

"When we suffer much we have a great chance to show God we love him. Julie, I have heard and read what you have been through, a great deal of suffering, and I ask why are you still here? Why didn't you leave the church? Why didn't you leave God? Because your spirituality is so powerful. It is far more powerful because of the things that you have been through and you have so much to teach me. I don't know how you did it. I really don't, but I'm in awe of you and I am in awe of your spirituality."

Father John Marsh - West Yorkshire England

"Your music, the songs written from the joys and sorrows of your life, are an integral part of the way you share your story and give convincing witness to the Lord Jesus. This book is a wonderful combination of the graced movements of your mind and heart. I pray it will inspire many others in their faithful following of Christ."

Bishop Thomas Olmsted - Phoenix, AZ

Theresa Gajeski, Father Battersby
and Julia Karas

MOST TALENTED, Jim Keenan and Julie Estel

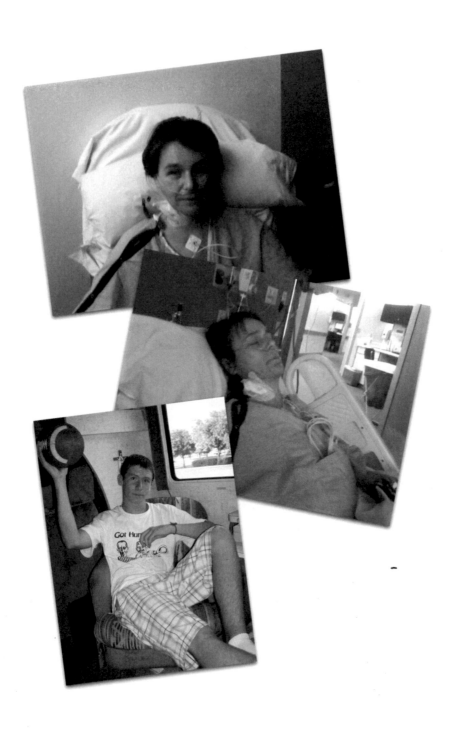